TORONTO'S

CHEAPER

EATS

July 2000

To
Lillian & David

Enjoy

Sara Waxman

3RD EDITION

TORONTO'S

CHEAPER
EATS

SARA WAXMAN

RAINCOAST BOOKS

Vancouver

Thanks to my daughter, Tobaron, and my son, Adam, for their inspiration and roadwork.

This edition © 2000 Sara Waxman

Raincoast Books
8680 Cambie Street
Vancouver, B.C.
V6P 6M9
(604) 323-7100

www.raincoast.com

This book was originally published in 1994 by Burgher Books.

1 2 3 4 5 6 7 8 9 10

Canadian Cataloguing in Publication Data:

Waxman, Sara, 1938–
Toronto's cheaper eats

Includes index.
ISBN 1-55192-308-4

Restaurants-Ontario-Toronto-Guidebooks. I. Title.
TX910.C2W38 2000 647.95713'541   C00-910090-3

Edited by Meg Taylor and Alicia Peres
Book layout by Bamboo & Silk Design Inc.

Raincoast Books gratefully acknowledges the support of the Government of Canada, through the Book Publishing Industry Development Program, the Canada Council for the Arts and the Department of Canadian Heritage. We also acknowledge the assistance of the Province of British Columbia, through the British Columbia Arts Council.

Printed and bound in Canada

Contents

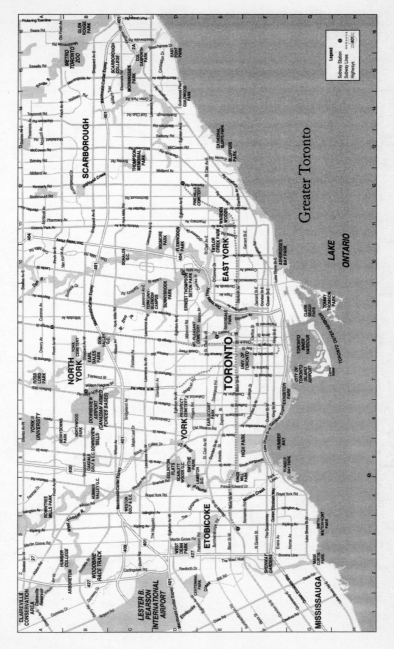

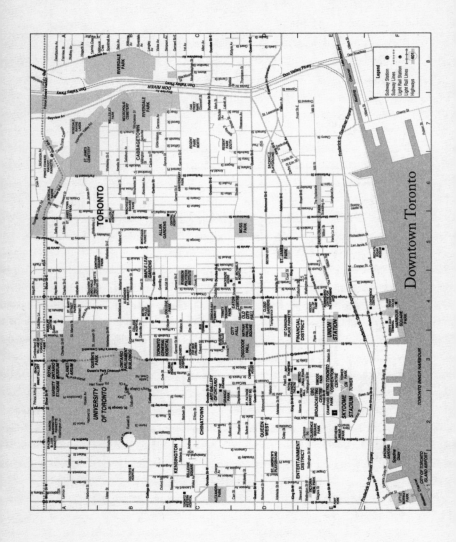

Downtown Toronto

Introduction

The Whims of Change

Our culinary landscape is painted in broad brushstrokes that shift
and evolve. We feel the ripple effect of world events as borders
change, peoples scatter, and immigration flourishes. Recipes travel
freely without passports, and suddenly, on Main Street, Canada,
there are restaurants offering the traditional dishes of distant lands.
Our abundant fresh produce, once exclusively filtered through
French, British, and Italian cooking techniques, now benefits from
the intoxicating spicing of Southeast Asia, the sweet and pungent
flavours of the Middle East, the soulful dishes of Latin America.

In the last few decades, Toronto's culinary landscape has under-
gone massive remodelling. We've come from being a spaghetti and
meatballs, chicken chop suey, roast beef and potatoes type of town
to the status of a world-class dining centre. Spend some time
wandering around the city. You might find yourself in Little Italy,
or in one of half a dozen different Chinatowns, or perhaps in Little
India or in the Greek area of town. You can indulge in Japanese,
Caribbean, Ethiopian, or Sri Lankan food. Or you may get swept
away by the veritable tidal wave of Korean, Vietnamese, Laotian,
Thai, and Malaysian restaurants.

Watch for the smaller restaurants, where the owner is also the
chef — allowing one person's food philosophy to touch every
aspect of the dining experience. Bistros, cantinas, taverns, trattorias,
tapas bars, pasta bars, wine bars, and cafés punctuate the traditional
dining scene. In some of these smaller restaurants, where cheaper
prices may mean "cozier" seating, you may find yourself dining
inches away from complete strangers. Relax, sit back, and enjoy the
scene — it's all part of the action.

In my continual search for perfect little out-of-the-way restaurants,
I can't help but notice a whole new generation of chefs. These
twenty-something culinary whizzes think globally. They cook with

the premise that every ingredient is in season — somewhere in the world — just hours away from landing in their sauté pan. It's from within these ranks that the star chefs of tomorrow will emerge.

Torontonians have high expectations, no matter where we dine. We can be a discriminating and demanding bunch. We want healthier and lighter foods — fish that were swimming yesterday, unblemished and perfectly cooked vegetables, green salads still damp with the morning dew. Luckily for us, most chefs and owners are of the same mind.

The restaurants have changed too. Spicy peanut sauce, hot salsa, and dipping sauces have become our mustard and ketchup. The small intimate bistro has become the standard of the times. Smart restaurateurs know that good food plus good value is still the formula for success — particularly in the restaurants listed here, where the food is delectable and prices are tempered with reason.

The Bill Is How Much?

Talking to some restaurateurs in the eighties, you got the sense that the customers were there to serve the whims of the chef. Today, there isn't an eatery in Toronto that doesn't bend over backwards to please. Surprising as it may seem, the average cheque for casual dining actually decreased in the late nineties, while fine dining increased less than $1 per person.

Try to peruse the menu with the eagle eye of the government reading your tax return. There are countless ways to shrink your bill without diminishing your enjoyment. Forget expensive mineral water. Live dangerously — ask for tap water with a slice of citrus. When ordering, be pleasantly explicit. There's so much that can go wrong within the ménage à trois of diner, waiter, and cook. Ask if you can split an order of pasta as an appetizer if the restaurant does not already offer pasta selections in two sizes. Appetizers that are priced over $8 are probably sizeable; two of these can make a substantial dinner for one person. Consider sharing a pizza as an appetizer. If you and your dining partner have both ordered appetizers, the restaurant may not mind if you split, say, a rack of lamb or a whole grilled fish between you as the main course. And what about dessert? A meal without dessert, some say, is like sex without a kiss. Since desserts have become such grand finales in this town, ask for one selection with two spoons. Before ordering a special kind of coffee, check the price. You might be surprised. Most good restaurants serve well-brewed regular coffee. Is a cappuccino or espresso really worth double or triple the price of a good cup of Java with refills?

The cost for dinner for two in all these restaurants is around $50. Of course, it depends what you order. Don't forget that a cooperative and obliging server should get a tip. An easy formula is GST + PST = TIP. And there you have it — the 15% tip on the pre-tax bill. Never, ever, be manipulated into tipping on the after-tax bill, and don't be embarrassed to reduce that 15% for a surly or condescending attitude. These days, however, most restaurant staff are hardworking, attentive, and genuinely hopeful that the people at their tables are having a good time. People talk. Happy customers tell their friends, but unhappy customers speak even louder.

Like a game of musical chairs, Toronto's restaurant scene is in a constant state of change. Chefs leave and new ones take their place, menus are revamped, restaurants close, hours of business may vary with the seasons. Fact is, we love it this way — there's no chance for boredom to set in. So, to avoid disappointment, it's always wise to call ahead.

The Evolution Continues

The doors swing in, the doors swing out. Since the first and second editions of *Cheaper Eats*, some of the cafés and bistros we recommended became so wildly successful and upmarket, they priced themselves right out of this book. In this third edition, all those that have closed or lost their relevance to this book have been deleted.

There are new restaurants, new menus, new concepts at every turn. Artisans and lighting technicians are making tiny dining rooms into unique environments, matching the personal statements of committed young chefs. Tables are inlaid with shards of glass and pottery, walls are camouflaged with handcrafted screens. Artists and ironworkers have teamed up to create stunning railings and door handles; halogen light, diffused through metal designs, throws intriguing shadows on floors and walls. And there's fusion cuisine everywhere. Even dyed-in-the-wool Italian restaurants on College Street are including a few Asian specialties in their repertoire. The New Asia trans-ethnic cuisine is the latest trend: Korean-Japanese, Lao-Thai, and dishes from Singapore and Vietnam are turning up on the city's smartest menus.

To check out the city's greatest culinary ventures, I have trekked from Etobicoke to Thornhill, from York Quay to Yorkville to North York, and discovered more than 200 restaurants (which you absolutely must try).

Bistro Tournesol
Pizza Tournesol

406-408 Dupont Street (at Howland)

TELEPHONE:
(416) 921-7766

CARDS:
Visa, Amex

HOURS:
Lunch:
Tuesday to Friday:
noon to 2 p.m.

Dinner:
Every day:
5:30 p.m. to 10 p.m.

Reserve a cozy table at this little outpost of Provence, under the vibrant art posters on sunny yellow walls. Displays of the signature bloom, the sunflower, lift the spirits. "Turn to the sun" is their name, translated. And Bistro, translated, should mean personal service, good bread, flavourful food, and impeccable frites.

It all comes together in their two-course fixed-price menu. Choice enough for the most financially challenged adventurers among us. Who could turn up her nose at wild rice pancakes served with smoked salmon capers and crème fraîche, or grilled eggplant wrapped around herbed ricotta cheese and baked in tomato sauce. Too fancy? There's Caesar salad or luscious steamed P.E.I. mussels. Eight second courses do tap dances with classic ingredients: sweetbreads pan-fried with madeira, fettuccine with three mushrooms, breast of free-range chicken filled with goat cheese and spinach. And yes, there are superb yam and potato frites, or, if you need nurturing, the homespun comfort of rosemary mashed potatoes.

Pizza is the king who lives next door. Keep your eyes on the pies and you'll note that two can share one of these extravagant beauties. With a salad, it's a meal.

The Bohemian

128 Pears Avenue (Avenue Road and Davenport)

TELEPHONE:
(416) 944-3550

CARDS:
All major credit cards

HOURS:
Tuesday to Friday:
4 p.m. to 2 a.m.

Saturday:
6 p.m. to 2 a.m.

Closed Sunday and
Monday

I love the comfortable rumpus-room feel of this neighbourhood spot. Non-structured, hand-decorated with unique flair, undemanding of fashion or fortune, it has quickly found its element. Twenty- and thirty-somethings lounge on comfy sofas, perch at the bar, or slide into booths and tables. Soon after young owners Phil Morrison and Stuart McKendrick opened this congenial spot, it became a venue of choice for Hollywood movie "wrap parties" after shooting a film in Toronto.

Veg out with salads: Caesar, Greek, or Grand Bohemian; add grilled chicken, ham, or beef; stack the salad with sprouts and eat it in a baguette. Falafel sandwiches, pizzas, and bruschetta are made with verve and served with all the panache the young Bohemian staff can muster. Five pool tables provide enough exercise to work off these easygoing and easy-eating light meals. Some people have been known to make this casual spot their second home.

Boulevard Café

161 Harbord Street (at Borden)

TELEPHONE:
(416) 961-7676

CARDS:
All major credit cards

HOURS:
Every day:
11:30 a.m. to 11 p.m.

(Kitchen closes at
10 p.m.)

For a change, a menu without pasta or pizza. For a change, the pungent flavours of Peru. Cumin and cilantro perfume dishes with names like Anticuchos and Mariscos al Vapor. On the cusp of the University of Toronto campus and the Annex, this cozy corner café fulfills the change of pace that we crave. Tables are bright ceramic tile. Hand-knotted wall hangings and banquette covers add to the warm, natural look. No glitz, no gimmicks, but plenty of glow. Homemade, dense corn bread is divine. Wine-doused oysters are crusted with toasty Parmesan. Whole chicken breasts are folded on skewers, charcoal-grilled, and served with a salsa of feta, coriander, and dill. Sea bass gets the same brochette treatment with a garlic and chili salsa. Salads have zip. Tropical juices like guava, passionfruit, and mango revive jaded taste buds, and the liqueur-laced coffees are heady. If you can, ignore the sometimes obtrusive voices of pompous academics who frequent the place, inhale the aromas that waft in from the kitchen, and pretend it's sunset in South America.

By the Way Café

400 Bloor Street West

TELEPHONE:
(416) 967-4295

CARDS:
All major credit cards

HOURS:
Every day:
11 a.m. to midnight

Bloor and Brunswick. At this "crossroads of the world" stands By the Way Café. Once a tiny "frogurt" booth (100,000 sold), By the Way has become a way of life for the Annex neighbourhood. Tune in to the conversations of liberals, radicals, capitalists, feminists, artists, young parents with babies, students, evangelists, vegetarians ... in short, an eclectic mix of big thinkers and big talkers. Days, sit at the window. Sip a bowl of café au lait; munch on a falafel or a pita filled with grilled cheese; nibble tabbouleh, baba ghanouj, hummus, and Middle Eastern finger food; or try a wholesome soup. Watch the world unfold. Nights, sit at the back and schmooze. Alas, even though a local artist has painted ecstatic chickens on the windows, you'll have to look mighty hard to find any in your chicken and avocado salad with sesame dressing. And as far as the Cajun chicken goes, why even the Colonel doesn't serve this part. Still, people-watching is high art, and a hearty meal is still affordable.

Dooney's

511 Bloor Street West (at Borden)

TELEPHONE:
(416) 536-3293

CARDS:
All major credit cards

HOURS:
Monday to Saturday:
10 a.m. to 2 a.m.

Sunday:
10 a.m. to 1 a.m.

(Kitchen closes at
11 p.m.)

On a hot Friday night, Bloor Street West could pass for any European city — it sure doesn't look like Toronto. For openers, people are out walking: the young and the old, the bold and the beautiful, the bad, the good, and the well-dressed (in that casual throwaway style that either happens naturally or takes hours to get just right). Where are they all going? At one point or another they'll end up at Dooney's. Some people prefer to sit inside. Air conditioning keeps it cool, and you can salivate over the vast display of desserts so sensual they should be x-rated. But the place to be is at a patio table, railside, watching the world pass by.

Order a glass of wine and crostini — grilled Italian bread slathered with either chicken-liver pâté or purée of smoked, roasted eggplant, then peruse the menu. I could make a meal of this lush crostini and a bowl of mussels steamed with tomato and basil and tingling with fresh chilis, piled on a slab of wonderful bread. People wait in line. Is it just for a table on the most popular patio in the Annex, or is it for the cold clam salad or penne verde with a purée of broccoli, garlic, chili, cheese, and a grilled sausage? On a busy night, the kitchen is harassed and slows to a crawl, but who cares when the food is tasty and you have a ringside table on life.

Dos Amigos

1201 Bathurst Street

TELEPHONE:
(416) 534-2528

CARDS:
Visa, MC

HOURS:
Tuesday to Thursday
and Sunday:
5 p.m. to 10:30 p.m.

Friday and Saturday:
5 p.m. to 11 p.m.

Closed Monday

So you don't know the difference between an ensalada and an enchilada, but you still want to partake of a Mexican fiesta on your plate? Enter here. Okay, so the entrance does not blow you away, but you can't eat architecture. Inside, warm and cozy are the buzzwords.

Start with a real Margarita, made with fresh lime juice (not something called bar mix) in a salt-rimmed glass. Order some freshly made guacamole, a mash of ripe avocado, onion, tomato, coriander and — wait for it — the unmistakable hot-flash of habanero peppers. If you always wanted to know what real taco chips taste like, you will get your answer.

This is Bathurst Street, where the streets are a feather away from being paved with chicken soup. The Mexican version is a full-bodied bowlful, afloat with hominy. They even make their own burritos here, with pork, beef, or chicken, and for pennies more it comes as a full meal with rice and salad.

Viva Mexicana, viva dos amigos!

Future Bakery & Café

483 Bloor Street West (west of Spadina)

TELEPHONE:
(416) 922-5875

CARDS:
Visa, MC

HOURS:
Every day:
7:30 a.m. to 1 a.m.

OTHER LOCATIONS:
2199 Bloor Street West
(east of Runnymede)
(416) 769-5020

561 Danforth Avenue
(416) 465-7705

735 Queen Street West
(west of Bathurst)
(416) 504-8700

There's nothing warmer on a blustery day than a big bowl of beef borscht, a schnitzel sandwich on dark rye with mashed potatoes and salad, or a buckwheat cabbage roll with mushroom sauce. This is the rib-sticking, soul-stirring, satisfying cooking of Eastern Europe, and its good vibrations are spreading faster than thick sour cream on a hot potato-and-cheese varenika.

What started as a bakery on Queen Street has blossomed into a small chain of stand-in-line cafeterias supplied by their own dairy.

Beloved by students for its generous portions, by homesick Europeans hungry for goulash and knishes, by chess players looking for a good game, by the cheesecake and coffee crowd, by health-conscious foodies looking for fruit salad with homemade yogurt and honey, by people-watchers looking for people worth watching. Future's is the best place to eat your heart out without emptying your wallet out. Alas, in some locations, they seem short on housekeeping staff.

Goldfish

372 Bloor Street West

TELEPHONE:
(416) 513-0077

CARDS:
All major credit cards

HOURS:
Every day:
noon to 10:30 p.m.

One goldfish in a pretty bowl, a tray of orange kumquats on a shelf, a spray of orchids in full and fragile glory. The facade is glass. It says come in, we live in a goldfish bowl and have nothing to hide. Looking out, the chrome-to-chrome Bloor Street traffic is like a moving urban mural, but inside the ambience is strictly cool. A cachet of breads comes in a square wooden box, along with three unique spreads on a ceramic tray set on a rivulet of pumpkin-seed oil.

Clearly, the kitchen loves the flavours of Southeast Asia, the substance of Italian pasta, the honesty of vegetarian culture. So, we are treated to a tower of roasted root vegetables crowned by curly strands of parsnip. And how does a warm goat cheese Napoleon stack up? Very nicely. Eggplant is layered with oven-dried tomatoes.

Pizzas are not a clone of what you would find elsewhere. Here, the crust wears duck confit, braised onion, and goat cheese, or a winning artichoke purée, roasted vegetables, and Taleggio cheese. In the relentless search for uniqueness, they have spiced gnocchi with cumin, angel hair pasta with galangal, and penne with hot peppery sambal.

But we forgive the confusion of this fusion when we dig into a big warm bowl of rice pudding that is rich with nubbins of dried fruits and cinnamon flavours.

Indian Rice Factory

414 Dupont Street

TELEPHONE:
(416) 961-3472

CARDS:
Visa, MC,
Diners/EnRoute

HOURS:
Lunch:
Monday to Saturday:
noon to 2:30 p.m.

Dinner:
Monday to Saturday:
5 p.m. to 11 p.m.

Sunday:
5 p.m. to 10 p.m.

In the sixties when the Beatles "discovered" India, anyone worth their flower-power jeans and love beads ran to dine in Indian restaurants. Among the first was Amar Patel's Indian Rice Factory. A suitably dim interior, utilitarian furnishings, and a resident mouse made us feel as hip as the hippest hippie. We cleaned our plates of vegetable pakoras, chickpea and tomato stew, and vegetable koftas, and imagined a kinship with the commune dwellers. The '70s, '80s, and '90s came and went.

Today, this restaurant has painted, polished, and cleaned up its act. The brilliant Indian pinks and greens are reflected in the glass panels, halogen lighting, and gleaming surfaces. Even the food has been so gussied up, it now includes trendy Chilean sea bass. Frankly, I think it's wise to stick to the tried and true. Lamb Toronto, a slow-simmered lamb shank in spinach curry, is pleasing, as are some of the vegetarian stews. And the kitchen's own ice creams are fruity and unusual. No longer a nostalgia trip, this is the look of the new and modern India.

Juice for Life

521 Bloor Street West

TELEPHONE:
(416) 531-2635

CARDS:
All major credit cards

HOURS:
Monday to Friday:
noon to 10 p.m.

Saturday and Sunday:
10 a.m. to 10 p.m.

There's more to life than the university class-room and more than one way to spend tuition money. This turned out to be a wise decision by the now proud owner of this funky juice bar and vegan café. She renovated and polished an old greasy spoon, kept the long narrow bar and small wooden booths, and created a menu that is representative of her lifestyle. To name just a few of the energy elixirs and smart drinks on the menu, there's Super Energy Cocktail, Einstein's Theory, Rocket Fuel Mix. Add a shot of wheat grass to any drink and you'll feel the blood coursing through your veins. An innovative three-page menu will amaze with its complex renditions of raw and cooked vegetables, brown rice bowls, hearty pan-Asian and Middle Eastern fare.

The Sunday brunch menu was one of the first to offer hemp-seed French toast and pair it with maple syrup and fresh fruit. A favourite is grilled corn and potato cakes with salsa. While waiting for a table at peak hours, you may need more patience than you can muster. Call ahead, if you can.

Kensington Kitchen

124 Harbord Street (west of Spadina)

TELEPHONE:
(416) 961-3404

CARDS:
All major credit cards

HOURS:
Sunday to Thursday:
11:30 a.m. to 10:30 p.m.

Friday and Saturday:
11:30 a.m. to 11:30 p.m.

"Where do you find these great places?" he asks as we leave the spacious tree-sheltered rooftop terrace. He'd never before had vegetable-stuffed baby eggplant, nibbled crunchy tabbouleh salad in an avocado, or dipped a hunk of warm whole-wheat pita into a plate of hummus. The owner, Said Mukayesh, has been serving fantastic Middle Eastern food for a decade at prices that give the wallet just a gentle nudge. Appetizers like stuffed vine leaves, fried eggplant, and baba ghanouj, and main courses like lamb burgers, meshwi, and meat brochettes, may sound too exotic for day-to-day palates, but the subtle blending of textures and seasonings — no hot pepper — is music to the mouth.

The décor is Age of Aquarius: painted wood floors, walls draped in Oriental rugs and cotton swatches. Up out of reach, a collection of hand-beaded purses. The kitchen, however, is strictly new millennium: big portions, intense flavours, low prices, and low fat.

Mumbo Jumbo

527 Bloor Street West

TELEPHONE:
(416) 531-5777

CARDS:
All major credit cards

HOURS:
Tuesday to Thursday:
5 p.m. to 11 p.m.

Friday and Saturday:
5 p.m. to midnight

Closed Sunday and
Monday

How do you know Mumbo Jumbo is cooler than the place you are hanging at now? Answer these questions: Does your current fave have a modern chaise lounge in the front window and some invitingly overstuffed sofas and chairs? Are there two TV sets over the bar playing a fifties colourized video (without sound) of *The Fly* starring Vincent Price or a black-and-white *The Defiant Ones* with an unbelievably young Sidney Poitier and Tony Curtis? And can you head to that bar between courses for a puff or two of that forbidden ciggy? If you're still not sure, go in, sit at a table along the banquette-lined wall, and order something.

The menu offers 20 choices from $5 to $19. All are big enough to share and many are finger-eatable. And surprisingly good. A baked portobello mushroom is plate-sized, stuffed with roasted red peppers and set on green salad; Insalada Yoko Ono makes a vegan happy; pizza is the sophisticated sensual cousin of "order in" pizza. Of course, there are sushi hand rolls four to an order, with a variety of fillings.

Everything from fresh oysters to steak and frites has appeal. And at the end, we welcome the complimentary vanilla and chocolate ice cream topped by fresh berries.

Nataraj

394 Bloor Street West (at Brunswick)

TELEPHONE:
(416) 928-2925

CARDS:
All major credit cards

HOURS:
Monday to Friday:
noon to 3 p.m.
5 p.m. to 11 p.m.

Saturday and Sunday:
5:30 p.m. to 11 p.m.

(Kitchen closes at
10:30 p.m.)

Among the potpourri of cuisines and thematic variations along the Bloor/Brunswick continuum, Nataraj offers an alternative. A dancing brass Shiva welcomes guests with open arms. Indian music wafts softly through a calm, gently toned interior, dishes are exciting yet comforting, spicing is subtle yet dramatic, and prices will bring joy to those with pecuniary concerns.

Behind a kitchen window, the chef shapes breads for the tandoor oven. Whole marinated cauliflower comes out red and steaming, and chicken, lamb, and shrimp are blessed with burst-in-the-mouth flavour. Hara kebab — spinach, cottage cheese, and potatoes mixed into small patties — are subtly seasoned; Dhingri Masala — mushrooms cooked with onion, tomato, and fiery spices — is smoothed with raita, a blend of yogurt and cucumber. Biryani rice dishes are fragrant with spice and textured with vegetables and nuts. There is nothing fancy here, but the loyal clientele likes it that way. Outside of a few ceremonial swords and statues, Nataraj has put money into cooking rather than décor.

Olive and Lemon

119 Harbord Street

TELEPHONE:
(416) 923-3188

CARDS:
All major credit cards

HOURS:
Every day:
5 p.m. to 11 p.m.

Award-winning filmmakers, broadcasters, designers, and food lovers congregate nightly in this celebrity roost. The signature dish is sautéed olives and lemons, both fruits from antiquity. Swipe a chunk of fresh bread through the warm oil and you are in for a taste thrill.

The reputation of the owners, Marlene and Giancarlo Carlevale (Trattoria Giancarlo on College, College Street Bar), draws the crowds. But reputation cannot camouflage the blinding sun and heat that comes in through the windows in summer and the icy blasts from the door in winter. Second-timers ask for a table near the bar.

Still, the food is wonderful. Dishes are restrained yet brim with exuberance. Plump grilled sardines are glorious; organic arugula in a lemony vinaigrette is sheer perfection. The back-to-basics spaghetti and meatballs is a winner, as is the crusty glazed whole-wheat rigatoni tossed with olives, pine nuts, and basil. Daily grilled fish and meats don't disappoint — desserts, however, do.

Le Paradis

166 Bedford Road

TELEPHONE:
(416) 921-0995

CARDS:
All major credit cards

HOURS:
Tuesday to Friday:
noon to 3 p.m.
5:30 p.m. to 11 p.m.

Saturday:
6 p.m. to midnight

Sunday and Monday:
5:30 p.m. to 10 p.m.

Love the joy of not cooking but hate restaurant prices? Le Paradis is authentic French bistro on a budget. Seven days a week, people come from the Annex and far beyond to savour dishes such as rabbit braised with fennel, tomato, and olives, or Moroccan braised lamb shoulder with couscous. To the staff, all diners are created equal, and all get the same casual service.

Since this 100-seat no-glitz neighbourhood bistro opened, it has attracted a loyal clientele of actors, writers, and producers — creative types who come to escape from the pressure of too many phone calls or the tragedy of not enough. Could be that dishes like Tajine de Volaille — a steaming stew that includes chicken, prunes, olives, and a shopping list of seasonings — get the creative juices flowing. And the prices are about what the arts community can afford these days. Sound too exotic? There's also steak and frites, and crispy herb-roasted chicken. Cool jazz and delicious aromas waft through the air, and though it's always crowded, you can actually hear what your friends are saying.

Serra Pizza Pasta

378 Bloor Street West (west of Spadina)

TELEPHONE:
(416) 922-6999

CARDS:
All major credit cards

HOURS:
Every day:
noon to midnight

(Kitchen closes at
11 p.m.)

Serra in Italian means hothouse, and this place is so hot that by 6:30 p.m. there's a lineup. Reason is, the food is fabulous. Thinly sliced fresh bread and a bowl of fresh tomato and basil salsa, a menu that reads like it just blew into town from New York or L.A., and prices about $3 less than they ought to be. Move fast. They may rise at any time.

Pizza is a fact of life. The idea of pizza is almost boring, but now, as the server places a big, thin-crust pizza in front of me, and the scent of smoked chicken, pesto, cherry tomatoes, smoked jalapeño, and mozzarella cheese wafts up to kiss my nose, I am regenerated. I look around and take note of my surroundings. A handsome flagstone floor, subdued "adult" lighting, pumpkin and ochre walls, a frantic open kitchen, and a long bar. Servers stay cool, polite, and friendly, even under pressure. Seats in front are a mixed blessing: a window on the passing Bloor Street parade, but a blast of frigid or hot air (depending on the season) as the door opens. Pastas are intriguing, but not large — but then again, neither are the prices. The salad of mixed field greens glistening with balsamic vinegar and virgin olive oil with crisp sun-dried tomato toasts is gorgeous, as are appetizers of mussels steamed in white wine and the house carpaccio. If you love tarte Tatin, order the superb apple tart with ice cream. Yes, life can still offer wonderful surprises.

True Grits

603 Markham Street

TELEPHONE:
(416) 536-8383

CARDS:
Visa, MC

HOURS:
Tuesday to Saturday:
5:30 p.m. to 10:30 p.m.

Closed Sunday and
Monday

How did crawfish get to New Orleans anyway? Legend has it that when the Acadians (Cajuns) left Nova Scotia for New Orleans, the lobsters followed, and the long trek wore their little feet down to nubbins. And how did Jambalaya get its name? "Jamb" (ham in Cajun French), "a la" in French, and "ya" (rice in African Creole). So what does midtown Toronto have in common with Louisiana? Three funky and fun Cajun/ Creole restaurants have opened in the same area.

They'll warn you in New Orleans not to wander off the beaten track at night, and if you're smart, you'll follow that advice. Alas, by doing so, you'd never find a restaurant like True Grits.

Start with sweet corn fritters or jerk chicken wings and a bourbon-based cocktail. You're on the case. Tuck into a side of barbecued ribs basted with molasses and bourbon sauce, or Southern fried chicken and gravy. Hot enough for you? If not, splash on some Pick-a-Pepper sauce or any one of many hot sauces. Name your poison. But save some room in your belly for a slab of pecan pie with two forks.

Via Oliveto

376 Bloor Street West (west of Spadina)

TELEPHONE:
(416) 925-6689

CARDS:
All major credit cards

HOURS:
Lunch:
Monday to Friday:
11 a.m. to 3 p.m.

Dinner:
Monday to Wednesday:
5 p.m. to 10 p.m.

Thursday to Sunday:
5 p.m. to 11 p.m.

From the outside, it looks like a simple Italian bakery that's open late. Once inside, the scene changes and it's a family restaurant that serves Italian-style food with a South American accent. Servers hail from Costa Rica and Nicaragua and the owner and his wife are from Argentina. Sometimes on weekends there's a little night music, maybe an operatic tenor serenading from a tiny stage in the corner.

After 9 p.m., the vegetables and pastas become a little tired, the server grows a little edgy, and the kids chase each other around the tables. But there's cheerful harmony from the kitchen in the early dinner hours, with home-style chicken cacciatore, a variety of pasta dishes, and a vast selection of antipasti including marinated calamari, artichoke hearts, lentils, and sun-dried tomatoes. Choose a combination of two or three. The best things here are the breads, tortes, pies, and cakes, made in the restaurant's own bakery a few blocks west.

La Bodega

30 Baldwin Street

TELEPHONE:
(416) 977-1287

CARDS:
All major credit cards

HOURS:
Lunch:
Monday to Friday:
noon to 2:30 p.m.

Dinner:
Monday to Saturday:
5 p.m. to 10 p.m.

Closed Sunday

La Bodega is a bistro pure and simple, with the most inviting summer patio on the street. Flowers, vines, and shrubbery entwine an iron fence, and tiny lights twinkle over the arch of the gate around this restored 19th-century house. There are no highs of discovery here, nor are there lows of disappointment.

Following the talents of the French chefs, they get a little fancy with their sauces. Seared filet of salmon has a maple glaze, breast of duck gets a call of the wild from blueberry sauce. Looking surreptitiously at the plates at neighbouring tables, I can see that most people come for the $19.95 fixed-price menu. For example, organic carrot and ginger soup, pan-fried boned trout served with the day's veggies, seasonal salad, and coffee or tea.

Remember La Bodega this summer when your mood is Canadian casual but your taste buds want something more romantic and French.

Café la Gaffe

24 Baldwin Street

TELEPHONE:
(416) 596-2397

CARDS:
Visa, MC

HOURS:
Monday to Friday:
11:45 a.m. to 11 p.m.

Saturday:
11 a.m. to 11 p.m.

Sunday:
4 p.m. to 10 p.m.

(Kitchen closes from
4 p.m. to 6 p.m.)

Around the corner from the AGO, on the cusp of Kensington Market and tucked into a storefront, is the casual, easygoing Café la Gaffe. Sincere as the church pews that serve as banquettes, it's filled with people discussing with gusto the last word in theatre, art, or politics. Some come to drink cups of Mocha Java, most come because they appreciate the food.

The open kitchen serves up hunks of garlic bread dripping with herbs and cheese, heaping platters of lime-sauced chicken brochette, grilled mahi-mahi, and crusty lamb chops. Daily veggies are scalloped potatoes, carrots and onion, stir-fried zucchini, and a cheese-topped baked tomato in big home-size portions. Seafood pizza is a deep-dish gourmet tap dance accompanied by a generous green salad. The chewy crust brims with lush ratatouille, piles of shrimp and squid, and a melt of mozzarella. Share a slab of fab chocolate cake for a sweet finish.

Cassis

168 McCaul Street

TELEPHONE:
(416) 979-0117

CARDS:
Visa, MC

HOURS:
Brunch:
Saturday and Sunday:
10 a.m. to 3 p.m.

Lunch:
Monday to Friday:
noon to 3 p.m.

Dinner:
Tuesday to Thursday:
5:30 p.m. to 10 p.m.

Friday and Saturday:
5:30 p.m. to 11 p.m.

A steady clientele comes home to Cassis for dinner so often, they're considered family. This clean and cheerful street-front eatery is an anomaly in the area. Neither ethnic, immigrant, nor student-focused cuisine, the menu evokes thoughts of fine dining in fancy restaurants. But there are no pretensions here; in fact, singles happily linger and read the daily papers after dinner.

The wild mushroom consommé "essenced with Riesling" is soothing as soup should be. Shredded five-spiced duck salad with julienned vegetables, drizzled with a Cassis reduction, is a house specialty. For me, these two dishes can make a meal, though they are in the section "To Begin." Eating right through into the "To Satisfy" section — and believe me, it does — I find the marinated salmon in edible papillote with new potatoes and orange-ginger beurre blanc. The cumin-coated lamb loin with vegetable couscous served in the curve of a crisp papadum and drizzled with mango glaze will tell you there is a fine chef at work in the kitchen. Of course, there are daily specials to delight vegetarians as well as carnivores.

Dai Nam Vietnamese Restaurant

221 Spadina Avenue

TELEPHONE:
(416) 598-3805

CARDS:
Amex

HOURS:
Sunday to Thursday:
10 a.m. to 10 p.m.

Friday and Saturday:
10 a.m. to midnight

Even though Vietnamese restaurants are popping up everywhere along a street that had become almost exclusively Chinese, know that the cuisine is totally different in style, seasoning, and technique. In the first place, it's low in fat content and high in flavour quotient. Refined cuisine is one of the few benefits Vietnam derived from the French colonial period.

One look at the menu-that-could-pass-as-a-catalogue and you will ask for guidance from a server. Pho is the mainstay. These luscious bowls of meat and noodle soups come with side dishes of crunchy fresh bean sprouts, sprigs of fresh basil, lime, and hot sauces. Add these and swirl them in the soup as you wish. Another tradition is what I call the roll-your-own. Order shrimp, vegetable, chicken, or whatever and get a platter that includes rice wraps, lettuce, vermicelli noodles, veggie strips, and peanut sauce. Look around, and follow what others are doing.

Fruit and vegetable milkshakes, like mango, avocado, or carrot, are refreshingly delicious. And what is French filter coffee with sweetened condensed milk if not a Southeast Asian latte?

Eating Garden

41 Baldwin Street (upper level)

TELEPHONE:
(416) 595-5525

CARDS:
All major credit cards

HOURS:
Monday to Friday:
11 a.m. to 3 p.m.
5 p.m. to midnight

Saturday and Sunday:
noon to 1 a.m.

It's a surprise to me that people don't line up around the block to get into the Eating Garden. Two-for-one lobster is always on special, and these bright red critters — chopped into manageable chunks and stir-fried with sliced ginger and green onion or black bean sauce — are sweet as can be. If the idea of fussing with lobster shells is beyond you, there are tiger shrimp with satay sauce served on a sizzling hot plate, or deep-fried prawns with lemon sauce. Fresh mango stir-fried with chicken makes a tasty combo.

Mr. Friendly Cheung, the owner, loves to cook, and his dishes have contemporary style and smart seasoning. With his wife, Debra, he has turned this into a cheery spot. Large paintings echo the pink and green floor and tables. High-backed black lacquer chairs add pizazz. Thick corn and diced chicken soup benefits from a tiny spoonful of hot pepper sauce or a splash of soy. Three kinds of sautéed mushrooms piled in the centre of a broccoli crown makes a stunning vegetable dish. Nothing is pre-cooked here; it's all made from scratch from fresh ingredients, so during peak hours there can be a wait between courses. But if you're in a hurry, Friendly can be convinced to cook a little faster.

ART GALLERY OF ONTARIO / CHINATOWN / KENSINGTON

Elixir

401 Spadina Avenue

TELEPHONE:
(416) 597-2915

CARDS:
Visa, MC

HOURS:
Lunch:
Tuesday to Friday:
noon to 2:30 p.m.

Dinner:
Sunday to Thursday:
5:30 p.m. to 10 p.m.

Friday and Saturday:
5:30 p.m. to 10:30 p.m.

Nothin' could be fina' than a stroll along Spadina. And do stroll, because parking your car is next to impossible. The nations of the world are homing in on this street, and to our delight, they're opening restaurants and cooking their traditional cuisines. Décor, at this point, is not a priority. Formica is okay and electric lights do the trick. We're here for the food of Persia, the kind of slow cooking that is labour-intensive and rich with herbs and spices.

Wonderfully seasoned vegetable soup or soup made of pulses like golden lentil. Curried lamb and fruit stews burst with complex flavour — I could make a meal of the fragrant basmati rice and some of this thick sauce. There is beef cooked with spinach, eggplant layered with fresh mint and dried goat cheese, chicken braised with cashews. These are the kinds of dishes served at dinner parties hosted by Iranians in their homes. Rarely is food of this quality found in a restaurant. To complete the meal, all we would need is a big bowl of fresh pistachios and dried seeds and berries on the table, and we could close our eyes and imagine we're eating in Teheran.

Happy Seven Restaurant

348 Spadina Avenue

TELEPHONE:
(416) 971-9820

CARDS:
Visa, MC

HOURS:
Every day:
11 a.m. to 5 a.m.

I enter Happy Seven and wait for my nose to give me the news: good or bad. The room smells fresh and airy. Good. As people leave, tables are immediately cleared — dishes are removed, then a layer of white plastic tablecloth is wrapped around the residue and carted to the back door. New place settings appear almost instantly. Servers walk the aisles between tables, explaining, suggesting, bringing dishes, clearing. No glamour: the money is in the kitchen, not the décor.

A server dips her tongs into the lobster tank, lifts out two lively ones, drops them into a large metal bowl and takes a short walk to the wok. Chopped and stir-fried, one with black bean sauce, the other with green onion and ginger. And you can always count on a dish called Buddha's Delight to give you a stir-fry of all the seasonal Chinese vegetables. Today, we all embrace tofu — especially when each block is stuffed with shrimp, then deep-fried. Sweet-and-sour beef tenderloin and chicken and pineapple chunks piled high in a hollowed-out pineapple are both keepers. At the end, there's a plate of sliced oranges.

Dance clubs and bars close at dawn, and so does this kitchen. In the hub of Chinatown, they're wheeling crates of fruits and vegetables out to the street. Spadina is coming alive again.

ART GALLERY OF ONTARIO / CHINATOWN / KENSINGTON

Kensington Café

73 Kensington Avenue

TELEPHONE:
(416) 971-5632

CARDS:
None; cash only

HOURS:
Monday to Saturday:
10 a.m. to 6 p.m.

Closed Sunday

The Kensington Market arts community congregates in this café — the perfect place to stretch your mind and sun yourself while the afternoon rays pour through storefront windows. Attractive rag-rolled walls and local art displays that change every few months add to the easygoing neighbourhood ambience. In the kitchen, the pasta has a creative bent as well. Fusilli with chicken and creamy garlic cheese sauce comes in red, white, and green, the colours of the Italian flag; a sandwich of capicolla, green peppers, and Brie does the same.

Vegetarians find plenty of excitement in penne with sweet peppers, black olives, and basil; a sandwich of avocado, Swiss cheese, alfalfa sprouts, cucumber, and tomato; and the Ultimate Veggie Lasagna (mushrooms, spinach, zucchini, eggplant), a generous portion of Caesar salad spilling over the plate, and chunks of warm garlic bread — all at prices that even our grandparents would find reasonable.

It's a personal environment, a small place but not cramped. Sure is nice to sit in the window, unchallenged, and watch the whole world go by.

Last Temptation

12 Kensington Avenue

TELEPHONE:
(416) 599-2551

CARDS:
All major credit cards

HOURS:
Every day:
11 a.m. to midnight

Kensington Market, where people moving to the ebb and flow of world events make a pit stop. Among them, enclaves of hippies, struggling students, chefs shopping with integrity, preppies from the suburbs buying torn jeans from secondhand stores on gold credit cards, and savvy restaurateurs and shopkeepers who've seen it all.

Last Temptation is a café named after a novel by Kazantzakis and owned by William Pham. Hummus with pita is smooth with a garlicky tang, green and white linguine primavera is generous and fresh, Oriental chicken or shrimp stir-fry sings of garlic or ginger, spicy roti is fresh and cooked with a light hand. Fresh fruit salad on yogurt is swirled with honey and cinnamon. A tiny price buys a main course with salad. And it's all served on white plates with blue trim, gold edges, and pictures of Hebrew tablets. Truly "melting pot" cuisine.

Lotus Garden Vietnamese Vegetarian Restaurant

393 Dundas Street West

TELEPHONE:
(416) 598-1883

CARDS:
None; cash only

HOURS:
Every day:
noon to 10 p.m.

In these days of uncertainty about what our food really contains, one thing is sure. More and more people are turning to vegetarianism. "I don't eat anything that has a face," say the vegans. They know why garlic and onion are not used and why an egg is permissible only during a full moon.

No MSG and little salt sullies the character of the produce used in this kitchen. Bowls of soup come in sizes large and larger; tofu in all forms is the ruler here. Tofu hot pot, for example, is well seasoned and one could even say rich with cubes of tofu, mixed greens, mushrooms, and all the veggies that are good for you. Flavours are so full you'll find yourself wondering if it's all an illusion.

This little gem is unlicensed, but the fruit drinks and shakes made from organic ingredients are so luscious and refreshing you won't even miss your usual glass of grape. Comes the revolution, there'll be a block of tofu in every pot.

Margarita's

14 Baldwin Street

TELEPHONE:
(416) 977-5525

CARDS:
All major credit cards

HOURS:
Monday to Friday:
11:30 a.m. to midnight

Saturday:
4:30 p.m. to 1 a.m.

Sunday:
4:30 p.m. to 12:30 a.m.

OTHER LOCATION:
229 Carlton Street
(416) 929-6284

A lighthearted Mexican cantina where the aroma of spicy cooking and the upbeat Latin music soundtrack make for instant relaxation. Summers, we can sip our triple Margaritas (there are five luscious flavours) on the upstairs patio, shaded by overhanging branches. Personally, I waffle between the fresh mango and the classic Margarita in a glass large enough to house a goldfish happily. Inside, ceiling fans turn lazily overhead. Mexican murals, guitars, a vicuña wall hanging from Peru, a blue and silver ceremonial sombrero, and a collection of Mexi-chotchkes adorn the walls.

In the kitchen, Eduardo and his cooks create a mean Mexican menu. Totopos, for example: a hot metal tray brimming with home-baked nachos, crumbled chorizo sausage, olives, sliced jalapeños, and melting jack cheese. The gua-camole is fabulous: a whole avocado is mashed in a porous stone mortar and topped with chopped raw onion, tomato, chili, and garlic. Eduardo's rendition of sizzling fajitas is the best I've had outside of Tijuana. A hot platter of stir-fried beef (or chicken) comes with all the fixings. Spread some red and green chili sauce on the just-baked tortillas, add a few lines of sour cream, a little chopped lettuce, a handful of grated cheese, sweet peppers, and top with the seasoned chunks of beef. There are Mexican beer and soft drinks chilling in an ancient blue refrigerator. This place makes me want to stamp my feet, clap my hands, and shout "Olé!"

ART GALLERY OF ONTARIO / CHINATOWN / KENSINGTON

New Ho King Restaurant

416 Spadina Avenue

TELEPHONE:
(416) 595-1881

CARDS:
All major credit cards

HOURS:
Sunday to Thursday:
11:30 a.m. to 4 a.m.

Friday and Saturday:
11:30 a.m. to 5 a.m.

A new touch at an old Cantonese restaurant: a Brita water filter pitcher brought to the table the moment you mention water. With this introduction, we're not surprised to find a light touch in the kitchen and a canny hand buying the groceries.

When was the last time you ordered classic chow mein? This is the place to revisit the dish that might have been your first encounter with Chinese food. If they're in season, order the baby leeks, stir-fried with beef, garlic, ginger, and black beans. Try chicken in a hot pot with stir-fried greens. At the end, in the Cantonese tradition, they'll serve the daily sweet soup — try it, it balances the meal.

Once, there was only one Chinatown in Toronto and the style of cooking was strictly Cantonese. Take your taste buds on a stroll down memory lane.

Southern Po Boys

159 Augusta Avenue

TELEPHONE:
(416) 593-1111

CARDS:
All major credit cards

HOURS:
Every day:
5 p.m. to 11 p.m.

Walk under the black-and-white canopy and through the heavy front door and y'all will think you've stumbled right into the South. It's a New Orleans Mardi Gras in Kensington Market. Here's the wrought-iron filigree look found in the old quarter of the city, and the tables spread with checked cloths. Upstairs, live bands and D.J.s serve up hot licks nightly. The signature dish is the Po Boy Sandwich. They say this sandwich was created during the Depression years on the Mississippi riverfront for longshoremen and working men ("poor boys"). The kitchen makes these with a generous hand and a Southern flourish. They fill a French baguette with roast beef, shrimp, or fried fish.

The menu lists all those Louisiana favourites we've heard about, but may not have had the opportunity to try. Fried green tomatoes, for example, or Jambalaya, or Andouille Chili with cornbread.

The owners of this happy spot love to party and they stay open 'til 1 a.m. when there's live music. A lighter, late-night menu delivers the same thrilling flavours. Oh, and don't leave without sharing a slab of New Orleans pecan pie.

Vanipha Fine Cuisine

193 Augusta Avenue

TELEPHONE:
(416) 340-0491

CARDS:
Visa, MC

HOURS:
Lunch:
Monday to Saturday:
noon to 3 p.m.

Dinner:
Monday to Saturday:
5 p.m. to 11 p.m.

Closed Sunday

"Come, eat rice!" (*Rappatan arhan!*) is the invitation to a Thai meal. Roving monks in Thailand carry wicker baskets on red cords, filled with sticky rice just like they serve at Vanipha. Pick up a small chunk with your fingers, roll it, then dip it into peanut sauce, soy sauce, nam pla fish sauce, or vinegared micropeppers. Eager to try Thai, but see danger lurking in chili? Relax. In this tiny below-the-stairs hideaway, chefs Vanipha, Ora, and Tnou prepare a sophisticated and refined Lao–Thai cuisine. They season gently with peanuts, coconut, lemon grass, cilantro, ginger, curry, and chili, and tone down the heat for palates not quite ready to make a quantum leap.

A pot of lively lemon-grass shrimp soup is enough for two. Try chicken stir-fry with a dozen sprightly vegetables, or mussels with Thai basil and onion, or fresh spring rolls of crab meat, shrimp, and veggie slivers. Each mouthful provocative and sensual. Just my cup of Thai.

Wah Sing

47 Baldwin Street

TELEPHONE:
(416) 599-8822

CARDS:
All major credit cards

HOURS:
Sunday to Thursday:
11:30 a.m. to 10:30 p.m.

Friday and Saturday:
11:30 a.m. to 11 p.m.

One small block of Baldwin between McCaul and Spadina is like a gourmet trip around the world: Chinese, French, Spanish, Malaysian, Vietnamese, Italian, Mexican — the list goes on. What brings me to this mealtime mecca is the two-for-one lobster specials. But I like this place for more than just the food. The tables are spacious, the room is scrupulously clean, service is courteous, and I love the electrical playthings on the ceiling, where pinpoint lights in a night sky change from red to green to yellow. Most days, a tank is filled with giant lively queen crabs ready to meet sizzling pan, ginger, and onion.

A pot of hot tea is our welcome. The maître d' tells us of the day's specials that include dishes to warm a vegan's heart. Fresh sweet-pea shoots, fresh watercress, stir-fried mushrooms (three kinds!), and watercress in a clear vegetable broth. Deep-fried oysters in crunchy batter with lemon are greasy ... but we love them anyway. Since my fortune cookie reads "You have ability to know and sense higher truth," I'll share my favourite menu numbers with you: #19 — giant fried shrimp, Szechuan-style (which leaves me breathless but happy), #57 — half duck with Peking sauce, #12 — two fried lobsters with black bean sauce, and, laying superstition aside, #13 — a duet of the same tender crustaceans, fried with ginger and green onion. "You order too much food!" says our server as he tries in vain to fit everything on the table at once.

Madras Express Café

1438 Gerrard Street East (at Ashdale)

TELEPHONE:
(416) 461-7470

CARDS:
Visa, MC

HOURS:
Winter:
Thursday to Sunday:
3 p.m. to 9 p.m.

Summer:
Tuesday to Friday:
1 p.m. to 9:30 p.m.

Saturday and Sunday:
noon to 10 p.m.

Closed Monday

The passage to Indian cuisine is filled with fiery flavours and exciting sights and sounds. Beautiful young women in bright silk saris and chiffon scarves, eating barbecued corn-on-the-cob; shops bursting with gilt fabrics, sequined slippers, and fine cotton shirts. The streets are crowded with people walking, chatting, and laughing, and everywhere there is food and the scintillating aroma of spices.

At Madras Express, a tiny take-out or eat-in café, the flavours will thrill you, and frankly, so will the cost. On a balmy summer's eve, claim a street-side picnic table under an umbrella and enjoy the passing parade of urban life. Step inside to order a masala dosa and prepare for a ride on a culinary roller-coaster. The dosa is a folded, foot-long, crunchy rice-flour pancake, filled with a saffron-gold potato and mustard-seed filling that sings with wonderfully clean flavours. Of the sauces, coconut chutney sends particularly lovely vapours to the nose. A bowl of vegetable-filled soup, sambar, is blessed with coriander and creates an agreeable balance of sweet and savoury. Share a dessert of kheer, a chunky pistachio and almond rice pudding, flavoured with cardamom. Scrumptious. There is no ambience to speak of, nothing chic or hip at this café — only food that will kiss your taste buds and win your heart.

Pulcinello Trattoria Napoletano

1590 Queen Street East

TELEPHONE:
(416) 463-5373

CARDS:
All major credit cards

HOURS:
Every day:
6 p.m. to 11 p.m.

The thick-crust pizza I ate in Naples plays in a different ballpark than Toronto's cracker-crust pizza. But to Neapolitans, it ain't pizza if it isn't chewy, with a good slathering of San Marzano tomatoes. We cut our teeth on the Southern Italian food of Naples. But in the last few decades, the hue and cry has been for Northern Italian food. How soon we forget the comfort food of the South. What goes around, comes around.

The mascot here is the sad clown of Naples, Pulcinello. But he can't bring down the mood. In this trattoria-style restaurant with red-and-white vinyl tablecloths (and cloth napkins), we're reintroduced to the food and joyous music of Naples and Campagna. Littleneck clams steamed with tomatoes and parsley; pappardelle with fava beans and prosciutto; mussels with basil, garlic, olive oil, and pasta. And there's usually a pasta with a rich meat ragu.

Of course, they have fresh fish, grilled, but that's the pricey part of the menu. Why bother when there's such great Neapolitan pasta on the menu?

Skylark

1433 Gerrard Street East

TELEPHONE:
(416) 469-1500

CARDS:
All major credit cards

HOURS:
Every day:
Lunch:
11:30 a.m. to 2:30 p.m.

Dinner:
3 p.m. to 10 p.m.

(Free delivery over $30)

Satisfied smiles are reflected a zillion times in two extraordinary walls of diamond-shaped mirrored wall tiles. From the minute you enter this pretty restaurant, the owner, Gurnam Multani, extends a jovial welcome. Take a seat at one of the tables draped in a bright blue cloth, and consider: buffet or menu?

The ten-item dinner buffet — at $7.99 — usually helps us to make up our mind. Just help yourself: mixed vegetables in sweet cream, cauliflower and potatoes in a spicy red Indian seasoning, and chickpeas and mung beans in a rich onion sauce. And there are also fresh vegetable salads. A vegan can feel secure in his required food groups here. The rest of us take a heaping serving of lamb curry, a few pieces of tandoori chicken, and Chicken Mughlai cooked in dried fruit sauce with intriguing Indian spices.

Just when we think we've found the bargain of the year, there is more. Mr. Multani strolls around offering hot naan bread freshly baked in his tandoor oven. This is surely the prettiest Indian restaurant in the area. No wonder it's stayed popular for 21 years.

Sunset Grill

2006 Queen Street East

TELEPHONE:
(416) 690-9985

CARDS:
None; cash only

HOURS:
Every day:
6:30 a.m. to midnight

Life is a beach — or is it the Beaches? To the "Beachers" who live in this old Toronto lakeside neighbourhood, shorts and sandals and a dog for walking are almost fundamental. So is the weekend brunch at the Sunset. There's nothing hokey or insincere about this traditional diner. If you walk beyond the few tables at the front, the service bar, and the open kitchen, you'll find a mezzanine with wooden tables and chairs that leads to a sky-lit, plant-filled room at the rear. After 10 a.m. on the weekends, the lineup snakes all the way to the street corner. So what's the attraction here? People come because the Sunset is an oasis of basic reality in a virtual-reality world.

All-day breakfasts — three eggs (any way you like 'em), a mountain of crusty home fries, slabs of buttered toast with jam, and bacon, sausages, or ham — are still under five bucks. The short-order cook moves at the stove as if choreographed: flipping thick French toast, nudging a huge veggie-filled omelette into a perfect oval, grilling hamburgers to order. Salads and homestyle desserts are generously portioned. Servers are as friendly as Mom when she's happy to see you, and they keep the coffee coming.

Tulip Steakhouse

1610 Queen Street East

TELEPHONE:
(416) 469-5797

CARDS:
All major credit cards

HOURS:
Every day:
7 a.m. to midnight

There's an urban legend that some people come into this restaurant in the morning for breakfast, stay around for lunch, and watch the passing parade on Queen Street until coffee break. Homemade pies are coming out of the oven. Then they walk around the block and return to get a great seat in a front booth or at the tiny counter in time for dinner. It's not hard to believe.

The all-day breakfast is the favourite meal for many. Who'd turn up his nose at a decent Western omelette, or a classic cheese? And the fab French toast comes with strawberry or apple topping with whipped cream and nuts.

The regulars know that on the first and third Tuesday of the month the daily special is Beef Stew, and that alternates with the second and fourth Tuesday — Corned Beef and Cabbage. They come from far and wide for the grilled steaks and chops: Porterhouse, Club Cut, and T-bones that are half the cost of steaks in a high-rent location.

A shock wave went through the community when they heard The Tulip was closing. It's true. "We're moving two doors west," says owner Sheila Lui, "it's bigger, brighter, and cleaner."

Whitlock's Restaurant

1961 Queen Street East

TELEPHONE:
(416) 691-8784

CARDS:
All major credit cards

HOURS:
Monday to Saturday:
11:30 a.m. to 11 p.m.

Sunday:
10:30 a.m. to 11 p.m.

The oldest free-standing all-wood corner structure left in the city is home to Whitlock's, and it's just as reliable and integral to the community as the handsome 1908 clapboard building.

Officially, it's the first restaurant in Toronto to make and sell true house wines, created especially for them by Magnotta Wineries in the Niagara region. But Whitlock's doesn't claim credit for creating a teriyaki chicken sandwich — there are versions all over town — made with marinated, grilled whole chicken breast between two thick slices of fresh egg bread with lots of lettuce, tomato, and cucumber, and a side of fries. They didn't invent the grilled chicken Caesar salad piled in a crisp tortilla basket, or the vegetarian lasagna bursting with spinach and ricotta cheese. And for the all-you-can-eat Sunday brunch buffet (which they didn't invent either), the neighbourhood clientele flocks to this unpretentious place. The menu is diverse, with everything from Greek salad to Malaysian stir-fry to breaded chicken fingers. Personally, I'll be back for the homemade carrot cake with cream-cheese frosting and really good coffee. The eclectic Beaches community is into fresh and yummy food, not dishes newly minted. No glitz or glam here, this big dining room has all the casual comfort of your favourite beach clogs.

Amber

2372 Bloor Street West

TELEPHONE:
(416) 763-6164

CARDS:
Visa, MC

HOURS:
Lunch:
Every day:
11 a.m. to 2 p.m.

Dinner:
Monday to Wednesday:
5 p.m. to 8 p.m.

Thursday to Saturday:
5 p.m. to 10 p.m.

If you wake up on a Sunday, hungry for a bowl of beet borscht plump with vegetables and a good dollop of sour cream, come on down. Think of it as a visit to your Baba's house for Sunday lunch. In fact, this is the kind of food you might get at Martha Stewart's Baba's house.

Would a big juicy cabbage roll filled with ground beef and rice, smothered with lots of oniony tomato sauce, and a dollop of mashed potatoes, give you a feeling that you have your feet on the ground? Two of you can share a family-style platter of hand-cut egg noodles and saucy beef stroganoff or rib-sticking beef-filled pelmeny dumplings with fried onions and sour cream. A properly done schnitzel can make your day. Boneless veal — flattened, breaded, and crisply fried — comes topped with a fried egg and sautéed mushrooms, or cheese and bacon.

The restaurant is small and tidy, decorated in shades of gold and yellow, and dark wood. Hand-painted plates and European chotchkes adorn the walls. It's as if the whole room was plucked from a Poland/Ukraine border town and plunked down in Bloor West Village. I admire some great-looking homemade cakes in the cooler but my brain says, "No room, no room!"

Bizou Bistro

416A Roncesvalles Avenue

TELEPHONE:
(416) 538-3626

CARDS:
Visa, MC

HOURS:
Brunch:
Saturday and Sunday:
11 a.m. to 3 p.m.

Dinner:
Every day:
5 p.m. to 10 p.m.

Summer patio:
11 a.m. to 10 p.m.

A small kiss (*bizou*) is an apt name for this impeccably turned out tiny bistro. Still, they've been thinking big. Affection and good taste seem to go hand in hand. The walls are hung with huge oil paintings: credible copies of familiar works by Toulouse-Lautrec and Gauguin, as well as a consignment of work by a local artist.

Almost all the shiny black tables are filled nightly by a local clientele, and the why of it is no mystery. When you can choose from a one-page menu that offers traditional as well as new flavour trends, as well as five vegetarian dishes with a French twist, the service is friendly, and the prices are right, why leave the neighbourhood? If we found the equivalent in France, we'd be lauding it to the skies.

The chef is from Anjou in France, and his skills are evident. The pungency of roasted beet vinaigrette lifts mixed green salad to new heights. Crispy root vegetable pakoras with fresh mint and coriander chutney and hot sauce drizzle is perfect for sharing. Canadian sirloin steak with Yukon Gold frites and roasted garlic aioli is a classic. And customers won't let them remove Coq au Vin (an old-fashioned French dish of chicken braised in Merlot with bacon and mushrooms) from the menu. When the charming summer patio opens, the ranks of guests swell from 34 to 100.

Blue Bay Café

2243 Dundas Street West (south of Bloor)

TELEPHONE:
(416) 533-8838

CARDS:
All major credit cards

HOURS:
Tuesday to Sunday:
5 p.m. to 10 p.m.

Closed Monday

Mauritius is just a dot on the map in the Indian Ocean, 20 degrees south of the equator. For some South Africans, it's Miami Beach, and it was also home to the now-extinct dodo bird. The Dutch, French, Arabs, Portuguese, and British have all passed through this island over the centuries, leaving a legacy of fiery French/African/Creole cuisine. Mauritians Marianne and Alain Lee (she serves, he cooks) have kept the Blue Bay's décor simple, the menu authentic — in the torrid-flavour zone — and heavily reliant on fish and seafood. Snapper swims in a wicked sauce of garlic, onion, and bright yellow mustard seed. Daube — a mouth-searing stew of chicken, peas, and potatoes — will leave you breathless. Or go for the burn with sautéed beef, tomato, and okra. Temper the heat with steamed rice and tiny ramekins of condiments such as chutney, greens, crushed onion, a dry yellow coleslaw, and simple red kidney beans. Cool mango sorbet for dessert is a lifesaver. Blue Bay is a favourite with the hot and spicy underground.

The Butler's Pantry Café

371 Roncesvalles Avenue (south of Dundas)

TELEPHONE:
(416) 537-7750

CARDS:
All major credit cards

HOURS:
Monday to Thursday:
9 a.m. to midnight

Friday:
9 a.m. to 1 a.m.

Saturday:
10 a.m. to 1 a.m.

Sunday:
11 a.m. to 11 p.m.

OTHER LOCATION:
484 Queen Street West
(416) 504-3414

This comfy, rumpled-looking café is busy all day. For late lunch, early dinner, or afternoon coffee, the neighbourhood declared the Pantry a real find, and has settled in, enjoying this tiny café's multiple personalities. As for décor, there's a king's ransom of flea-market teapots and cookie jars perched on shelves. A room at the back is reserved for smokers only. Some days, our server sports lacquer-red hair, a tiny red-and-white tennis dress, and thigh-high stockings to match.

The menu is a hodgepodge of goodies, a cavalcade of culinary favourites: you can make lunch or dinner of anything from a toasted bagel with cream cheese and onions to spicy Jambalaya. Whatever the entrée — pasta with homemade tomato sauce, shepherd's pie, or spinach nut casserole with cheese — it comes partnered on the plate with a pile of sprightly salad. Even bulgogi, a Korean beef dish, comes with salad. After a vintage film at the nearby Revue Cinema, really good café au lait in a bowl with a warm raisin scone, lots of butter, and a few spoonfuls of jam hits the spot. And they make a great tuna sandwich, too. But when the kitchen attempts too many culinary cartwheels, it can slip up — an underbaked and underseasoned zucchini pancake, for example. A peek into the dessert display case will make you admit that you can't really go home until you've had a buttery Nanaimo bar or chocolate pecan square.

Crown Oyster Café

2253 Bloor Street West (west of Runnymede)

TELEPHONE:
(416) 760-0816

CARDS:
All major credit cards

HOURS:
Every day:
5 p.m. to 11 p.m.

Candy is dandy, liquor is quicker, but a platter of oysters and a glass of chilled white wine is the true aphrodisiac. So says my friend who makes a study of these things. At the Crown they set the tone with marina art on the walls and a red carnation and glass hurricane lamp on each marble table. They're big on mood illumination: I love the pink blocks of face-flattering ceiling light, and the blacklight in the rear dining area highlights white fabrics so that we literally glow with goodness.

Service here is meticulous, a portent of pleasant things to come. Malpeque, Pine Island, Aspy Bay, and Martha's Vineyard oysters, listed by size and price, are nestled on a metal tray filled with ice and seaweed. We dabbled with danger in the form of Hot Sauce from Hell, White Boy Soul Sauce, and Johnny Reb Espanola Sauce, to name a few. The caring kitchen offers two sizes — piccolo or grande — of most dishes, but there's nothing tiny about the piccolo. Oyster Slapjack is a satisfying, savoury stew; creamy risotto with large shrimp, squid, scallops, and mussels cascades out of a peppery papadum horn of plenty and shares the plate with a colourful vegetable stir-fry. Not sold on seafood? There's sliced veal bavette steak with mashed potatoes, sesame-stuffed chicken breast, and more. The bill comes with a lollipop for each of us, underlining the fact that the cost of a meal here is child's play.

Fiasco Trattoria

2279 Bloor Street West

TELEPHONE:
(416) 766-9961

CARDS:
All major credit cards

HOURS:
Monday to Friday:
11:30 a.m. to 11 p.m.

Saturday and Sunday:
10:30 a.m. to 11 p.m.

OTHER LOCATION:
Zsa Zsa
2277 Bloor Street West
(416) 766-7714

If you believe you need a sense of humour to get through life, giving a restaurant a name that means disaster is a good start. Reading the fine Italian writing intertwined with the grapevines and curlicues on the menu gives me a clue. Loosely translated: "What a stupid thing! Is that your husband? What a stupid thing!" In one word: Fiasco.

Satisfied that failure has nothing to do with the food, we're ready to relax under the retractable skylight in this long, narrow room. We dig into a plate of crispy, deep-fried coconut shrimp with curried marmalade, then share a pizza with wild mushrooms and three cheeses. A lively, casual crowd is loyal to this neighbourhood spot, and it's easy to see why. Service is friendly and the menu offers a non-intimidating culinary trip around the world. Pastas are piled high with combinations that would astound a purist but delight an adventurous palate. Fettuccine with chicken, tiger shrimp, fresh oranges, and snow peas in creamy Cointreau sauce, for example, speak eloquent Esperanto. And the big delicious home-baked pies and good coffee are no joke. Sister restaurant Zsa Zsa next door offers a similar menu from a shared kitchen and is equally worth the visit.

Queen's Pasta Café

2263 Bloor Street West (west of Runnymede)

TELEPHONE:
(416) 766-0993

CARDS:
All major credit cards

HOURS:
Lunch:
Monday to Saturday:
noon to 3 p.m.

Dinner:
Monday to Thursday:
5:30 p.m. to 10 p.m.

Friday and Saturday:
5:30 p.m. to 10:30 p.m.

(Kitchen closes from
2:45 p.m. to 5:30 p.m.)

Sunday:
5:30 p.m. to 9:30 p.m.

OTHER LOCATION:
Queen's Pasta Take-Out
(to cook at home)
256 Beresford Avenue
(416) 259-7201

How do you spell pasta? At Queen's Pasta Café, they spell it many ways. Linguine with chicken in a sun-dried tomato and garlic cream sauce; penne tapenade with black and green olives, artichokes, hot chili peppers, and garlic; and even plain spaghetti with tomato sauce. It's a charming, turquoise and black, window-lined corner café, where family and food are important. Black-and-white photos line the walls: babies, grandparents, and a bunch of guys who look like anybody's uncles, fishing. Healthy plants hang from the ceiling, swaying slightly in the breeze from ceiling fans. The look is modern but not glitzy; comfortable but not careless. Well-mannered servers work with alacrity. Refills of bread and butter, half orders of pasta at lunch, and a good knowledge of the menu are things I appreciate.

But there's more to this café than just pasta. Caesar, Greek, and garden salads; satisfying sandwiches of pan-fried breaded veal on Calabrese bread with sweet peppers or spicy Italian sausage with hot banana peppers (alas, only served at lunch). At dinner, a little more sophistication sets in with Veal Parmesan and linguine with shrimp creole, for example. Still, the style of this place is friendly and easygoing. Trouble with eating all this good Italian cooking is that, five or six days later, you're hungry again.

River

413 Roncesvalles Avenue

TELEPHONE:
(416) 535-3422

CARDS:
Visa, MC

HOURS:
Tuesday to Friday:
11:30 a.m. to 10 p.m.

Saturday:
5 p.m. to 10 p.m.

Brunch:
Saturday and Sunday:
11:30 to 3 p.m.

Closed Monday

With architectural design and whimsical creativity, they've created a wood-and-steel restaurant that actually has movement and flow. From the door handles to the elegant wooden cut-outs on the ceilings and the highly polished wood floor, there exists in this place a unique sense of nature and motion.

The warm spinach salad, for example, is a toss-up of baby leaves, caramelized sweet potato, roasted red peppers, toasted walnuts, and Asiago cheese, splashed with a warm honey-balsamic dressing. Splendid sandwiches all come with roast curry potatoes, soup, or salad. Hey, we're on Roncesvalles, we've got to have perogies. For the '00s they're stuffed with shiitake mushrooms, braised cabbage, and tofu. And there's diversity: Thai noodles and grilled tandoori salmon.

Later, I learn that this design concept is no accident. River is a job-training centre for street youth who are being mentored by a professional Toronto chef. All Aboard Youth Ventures, a non-profit organization, is partially funded by Human Resources Development Canada.

Episode Café

195 Carlton Street (at Ontario)

TELEPHONE:
(416) 921-1255

CARDS:
All major credit cards

HOURS:
Lunch:
Wednesday to Friday:
noon to 3 p.m.

Dinner:
Every day:
5 p.m. to 10 p.m.

This groovy little café became such a magnet for the dual-income couples who live in this renovated enclave, they've had to expand three times in two years. Now, in addition to the long wooden bar that traverses the main dining room, there's a no-smoking fireplace room, an outdoor patio, a courtyard, and an herb rock garden. What has not changed is the warmth of the welcome. Regulars stop in for cappuccinos or just to schmooze, tucking briefcases under sturdy wooden chairs. They say it reminds them of Greenwich Village in the fifties and sixties.

The menu is all about choices and a new definition of comfort food. She's a vegetarian: baked polenta with Gorgonzola, roasted peppers, and sun-dried tomatoes or grilled portobello and oyster mushrooms on greens with shaved Asiago cheese. No cheese? No problem. He's looking for Asian adventure: pad thai rice noodles are piled high with chicken, shrimp, bean sprouts, and peanuts; somen noodles are plump with gingered beef, mushrooms, and tamari sauce; and the Japanese hot pot is a voluptuous mix of seafood in a dashi broth. Or maybe they just want a basic Canadian dinner: salad and pasta. You can't go wrong with the penne served with spicy garlic sausage or the peppercorn fettuccine with mushrooms and Jack Daniel's cream sauce. The owner serves, pampers, and feeds his neighbourhood, heroically. His medal should be in the mail any day now.

CABBAGETOWN

Tapas Bar

226 Carlton Street (west of Parliament)

TELEPHONE:
(416) 323-9651

CARDS:
All major credit cards

HOURS:
Lunch:
Friday:
noon to 3 p.m.

Dinner:
Friday and Saturday:
5 p.m. to 1 a.m.

Tuesday to Thursday
and Sunday:
5 p.m. to 11 p.m.

Closed Monday

In Spain, the Latin lifestyle says "Sí! Sí!" to tapas at 8 p.m. and dinner at 11 p.m. Here, we're on heavy-duty "daylight savings time," and so an exuberant and diverse crowd starts filing in much earlier, filling the cheery red-check-clothed tables and sharing fruit-filled pitchers of sangria. The focal point is the bar, hung overhead with bright orange Serrano hams.

You can while away many a happy hour here, eating as much or as little as you want from an appetizing selection of over 30 "little dishes" (tapas), homemade chorizo, or a good-size plate of prosciutto Serrano. There's also garlic shrimp in a tiny clay casserole, lentil soup with chunks of sausage and potato, spareribs, crispy squid or squid simmered in its own ink, and marinated salads. Later, when the music — with allegiance to Latin rhythms — gets louder, some spirited souls are moved to dance in the aisles, a signal for servers to join in the fancy footwork. That's why they were hired, after all.

CABBAGETOWN

Timothy's Chicken

556 Parliament Street (at Wellesley)

TELEPHONE:
(416) 964-7583

CARDS:
All major credit cards

HOURS:
Monday to Friday:
11 a.m. to 10 p.m.

Saturday:
noon to 10 p.m.

Sunday:
4 p.m. to 10 p.m.

(Delivery available
about an hour later
than dine-in)

Timothy's is famous not only for its tandoori chicken. There's chicken rubbed with Indian spices and grilled or diced and deep-fried in batter. It comes curried, gingered, barbecued, "Timmycued" (in the style of Madras), vindaloo- or jalfrezi-style. You can have it in a sandwich, salad, or soup, or in a barbecued chicken-and-rib combo.

But there's more fare to this tiny rose-coloured 30-seat café than fowl. Service is pleasant and helpful and, though some like it hot, requests for mild spicing are met. A hearty bowl of mulligatawny soup flavoured with fresh coriander and lemon comes with naan bread, hot from the oven. Vegetable pullao of baked fragrant basmati rice with diced vegetables and a choice of eight lavishly sauced vegetarian plates are simply priced. Traditional lamb and shrimp dishes will tempt you on occasion, but you'll be back for the addictive marinated and charcoal-baked Tandoori Dinner — a quarter chicken with naan and salad, fries, baked potato, or rice. The regular clientele from Cabbagetown and beyond keep the kitchen busy with take-out and delivery, one of the reasons Timothy's has been in business for over ten years.

The Town Grill

243 Carlton Street (at Parliament)

TELEPHONE:
(416) 963-9433

CARDS:
All major credit cards

HOURS:
Lunch:
Monday to Friday:
noon to 2 p.m.

Dinner:
Monday to Thursday:
5 p.m. to 10 p.m.

Friday and Saturday:
5 p.m. to 11 p.m.

Closed Sunday

A certain *je ne sais quoi* keeps the Cabbagetown neighbourhood regulars coming back to the community-oriented Town Grill. The smooth-as-silk crème brûlée? The frankly comfortable, "no problem" ambience? It's all this and more. The French-bistro cooking is authentic and good. The ever-changing menu card offers multiple choices of soups or salads and main courses. You might start with curly endive salad or leek and potato soup; proceed to choices that may include bavette steak and frites, calf's liver with pepper sauce, or grilled salmon with a buttery tarragon sauce. Finish with chocolate mousse. From the regular menu, the steak and frites is the same as you'd get at a side-street bistro in Paris. The difference between Cabbagetown and Paris, however, is that here, the waiter and the prices are much friendlier.

Kubo

155 Dalhousie Street (Merchandise Building)

TELEPHONE:
(416) 366-5826

CARDS:
All major credit cards

HOURS:
Monday to Thursday:
5 p.m. to 10 p.m.

Friday and Saturday:
5 p.m. to 11 p.m.

Closed Sunday

What's in a name? Do you feel confidence in the kitchen when you peruse the menu in a smashing new condominium building's style-possessed, wham-glam, pan-Asian restaurant/bar and you read Ooh Baby! Baby Green Salad or Sexual Hagrassment Lemongrass Lentil Soup or Fu Manchu With Love Tofu Stir Fry? What are they selling here, anyway?

Whether this menu makes you smile or wince probably depends on your age and your mood. The youngish, smartish, cell-phone-toting clientele are definitely in their element here. But fun and pun aside, some of these dishes are good. Motley Stew Red Wine Beef, for example, is given a Chinese persona and served in a bowl of rice with chopsticks. And the breast of crispy skinned duck comes in a rice bowl as well, with stir-fried greens and hoisin sauce.

Never judge a dish or a flower by its name. A rose is a rose is a rose — and we all know the complex beauty of it. So what if the menu lists "What the Duck." Who knew it would be such a tasty morsel?

Slack Alice

562 Church Street

TELEPHONE:
(416) 969-8742

CARDS:
All major credit cards

HOURS:
Monday to Wednesday:
4 p.m. to 1 a.m.

Thursday to Sunday:
11 a.m. to 1 a.m.

Someone here has an ironmonger in the family. The wrought-iron lettering outside, the half-moon chair backs and candles flickering in an ornate ironwork chandelier. Maybe the Latin words printed on velvet banquettes tell the tale. Alas, I am unilingual.

But what I do understand is friendly service, without a hint of attitude. And what I appreciate is a hearty bowl of made-from-scratch, seasonal vegetable soup like chunky tomato or lentil and carrot, salads composed of crisp fresh ingredients, and thin-crust pizza with healthy vegetable toppings. Daily specials of homestyle cooking make this kitchen a haven for lonesome doves.

Evenings, the pretty bar with its backlit diffused illumination is a popular meeting place. In summer when the French doors open to the street, it's hard to tell where to draw the line.

Spiral

582 Church Street

TELEPHONE:
(416) 964-1102

CARDS:
All major credit cards

HOURS:
Lunch:
Wednesday to Sunday:
11:30 a.m. to 2 p.m.

Dinner:
Every day:
5 p.m. to 10:30 p.m.

In summer, the rear garden seems especially pretty, and so does the clientele. Tiny lights twinkle in trees, flickering bamboo torches give complexions a refreshed, rosy glow. A century ago, this was an elegant family home. In winter, we can imagine the coziness of a bygone era as fireplaces crackle and polished old floorboards squeak.

Our waiter explains, with earnest cheerfulness, the nuances of tea-smoked quail stuffed with Vietnamese sausage and perched on a ginger-vinaigrette-splashed watercress nest. He extols the virtues of Thai chili-grilled calamari.

Fusion is the story here, and they are sticking to it. Pork tenderloin gets happy with Vietnamese spicing. Bright green baby bok choy and drizzles of ponzu sauce lift this dish way above the average. Good dessert chefs dream in technicolour and produce razzle-dazzle dishes like Havana Banana, a stack of sweet sugar cookies, layered with caramelized banana and pastry cream, set in swirls of chocolate and malted milk sauce.

Youki

4 Dundonald Street

TELEPHONE:
(416) 924-2925

CARDS:
All major credit cards

HOURS:
Tuesday to Thursday:
5:30 p.m. to 10 p.m.

Friday and Saturday:
5:30 p.m. to 11 p.m.

Closed Sunday and
Monday

Youki is off the beaten track — unless of course your track includes the cusp of the Church/Wellesley gay village. No matter, the siren song of satays, sushi, and searing Asian pickles has people dropping in from the outer limits. In summer, there are prized terrace tables, the better to sit and watch the evening's passing parade. In winter, we like the cozy homespun and wood interior, and the glazed pottery serving plates remind me of restaurants in Japan.

This 40-dish menu has us totally fooled. With such low prices, you'd expected small tastings. Not so. Grilled eel sushi comes in a set of eight; lobster and avocado sushi with scintillating pickled ginger and devilish wasabi is the same; and there are grilled grapeleaf-wrapped portobello mushrooms folded into rice paper. Try to do justice to a Southeast Asian menu after this! These are not your standard backyard barbecue ribs, says the rib maven, euphoric over the delicious flavour explosions of Indonesian spicing. Grilled salmon glistens with teriyaki glaze; and kingfish, golden with turmeric and lemon grass, comes tightly wrapped in a banana leaf.

Dine-alones head for the sushi bar, sipping a glass of muscat and watching the chefs make magic with exotic ingredients. Better than watching the food channel — and here you get a tasty payoff.

Bar Italia

582 College Street

TELEPHONE:
(416) 535-3621

CARDS:
All major credit cards

HOURS:
Every day:
11 a.m. to 11 p.m.

(Drinks to 1 a.m.
on weekends)

It isn't easy owning an Italian restaurant on a street that's chock-a-block with Italian restaurants. So why is it that this sassy spot is always jumping?

The room itself is as plain and sleek as an Armani suit. Leather-like booths where even six good friends can squeeze in comfortably, marble-topped small tables in the main dining room, and a long bar for schmoozing, sipping, eating, or meeting. A few rows of hanging lamps illuminate the tables and the food. In the front, the puffers who sit nursing their drinks look as if they were planted there by a film-casting company.

Inside, it's *la dolce vita* — the good life. Al dente bowls of pasta, five to choose from. I like the fettuccine with smoked salmon or capellini with grilled sausage and herbs. Salads amaze with their choice elements: sautéed mushrooms, arugula, sliced Parmigiano and toasted walnuts or thinly sliced air-dried beef with Boston lettuce, endive, and avocado; grilled panini sandwiches of chicken, goat cheese, and other yummies; warm pork loin with avocado and strips of pancetta.

And who can argue with good house wine, gently priced. The early dinner crowd melds into the late-dinner hordes, and the night prowlers usually close the place with lattes and cappuccinos in the wee small hours.

Café Societa

796 College Street

TELEPHONE:
(416) 588-7490

CARDS:
All major credit cards

HOURS:
Dinner:
Every day:
6 p.m. to 10 p.m.

(Drinks to 2 a.m.)

Go west on College Street, way past what you'd consider the usual landmarks, cross Ossington, and you're getting close to the just-hatched hip, hot area. The new restaurateurs, the ones who haven't proven themselves yet and have more enthusiasm and dreams than they have hard cash and experience, are going as far west as it takes to find reasonable rents. Like farm teams for the NHL, these are the chefs the big boys watch.

Here's Café Societa, a pastel-painted labour of love. So what's cooking here? A table of six regulars dig into individual bowls of linguine with smoked chicken and Gorgonzola cream sauce, and herb pappardelle with shrimp, corn, fresh tomato, and truffle broth. Salads are made with organic lettuce tossed in maple, apple cider, and pumpkin-seed oil vinaigrette, sprinkled with nutty toasted pumpkin seeds. Main courses of fish and chicken are paired with entertaining sides: a wedge of Oka cheese and pumpkin gratin, for example.

Go before everyone finds out about it.

The College Street Bar

574 College Street (at Manning)

TELEPHONE:
(416) 533-2417

CARDS:
All major credit cards

HOURS:
Monday to Friday:
5 p.m. to 2 a.m.

Saturday:
11 a.m. to 2 a.m.

Sunday:
11 a.m. to 1 a.m.

College Street has invented itself into the ephemeral thing that Yorkville was to the seventies and Queen Street West was to the eighties. This is the new bohemia of the '00s. Writers, actors, producers, directors, poseurs, artists, young beauties of every gender. There is much kissing and hugging in greeting. Much table-hopping. And some of the tastiest, cheapest food I've come across in a long time.

"Another order of Roman bruschetta, please," we call out as we catch the eye of the server in charge of the front half of the room. When the Metropolitan Cinema disgorges its audience, a crowd piles in, filling two refectory tables near the front windows. This place is already jammed with film buffs just in from a nearby screening.

The addictive bruschetta is four linebacker-size slabs of grilled bread, slathered with olive oil and liberally coated with coarsely ground black pepper. Large plump olives, sautéed with fresh thyme and sweet onions, leave us wanting more. I pass on the grilled sardines — today's catch is frozen, not fresh. Two rounds of grilled polenta are smothered under a lavish sauté of mushrooms and herbs. Rigatoni with asparagus and lemon comes in a soupy cheese sauce more suitable to linguine, but we love it anyway. Squid is grilled and splashed with olive oil, lemon, and oregano. Mediterranean flavours run rampant. Of course, there is tiramisu, ice cream, and coffee.

52 Inc.

394 College Street

TELEPHONE:
(416) 960-0334

CARDS:
Visa

HOURS:
Tuesday to Saturday:
5 p.m. to last call

Sunday:
noon to midnight

Closed Monday

Responsible consumption can be good business. Two young women opened their café, community hangout, handcrafted clothing and jewellery emporium with this in mind. They offered reading material that you wouldn't find in the public library and a blank-page book for comments in word or design.

The furnishings and fixtures, all spanking clean and polished, were rescued from the wrecking ball. And what did they serve at the tables and small bar? Only cold food, dips, sandwiches, salads, and hot soups. My guess at the time was that their culinary skills were limited, but their enthusiasm and charm was boundless.

Meanwhile, the partners have learned to cook and expanded their repertoire to include a really good menu and some evening entertainments. You're going to love this unique spot.

Giovanna Trattoria

637 College Street (at Grace)

TELEPHONE:
(416) 538-2098

CARDS:
All major credit cards

HOURS:
Every day:
11 a.m. to 11 p.m.

Like a dimple on the hip of the CHIN building, Giovanna Trattoria is a delicious addition to a street where almost every door opens to a good kitchen, a patio, and a wood-burning oven.

The city's obsessed gourmets have claimed this place as their own — and who can blame them? Caprese salad of ripe tomato slices and fresh bocconcini cheese on soft lettuce fills the dinner plate; Genovese salad (tuna, hard-boiled egg, green beans, tomato) is a meal with a basket of bruschetta and crostini; and the olive oil is extra-fine, extra-virgin. There's a lot of home cooking and love coming from the open kitchen. The owner, Giovanna, is at her best with the sophisticated peasant food we love. Polenta as a partner to lamb is divine; fusilli with chickpeas, chilis, prosciutto, and tomato is a winning combo. But I'll return like a kid to the candy store for the house specialty — Pollo Panzanella. A half chicken is roasted with herbs to crispy-skinned goodness and set on a traditional salad of chunky bread croutons tossed with coarsely chopped vegetables and herbs that have been marinated in a lush vinaigrette. Desserts — tiramisu, of course, and chocolate lemon semifreddo — are big enough for sharing, or try a glass of dessert wine with almond biscotti.

Kalendar Koffee House

546 College Street

TELEPHONE:
(416) 923-4138

CARDS:
Visa, MC,
Diners/EnRoute

HOURS:
Monday to Friday:
11 a.m. to midnight

Saturday and Sunday:
10:30 a.m. to 11 p.m.

Napoleon and Josephine would have loved this cozy, candle-lit salon. True grandeur, albeit on a small scale. Walls are a deep red; the ceiling is painted in the French Baroque manner with a circle of vines and flowers. A big old copper espresso maker adds character to a coffee service nook. Imagination runs rampant in the kitchen, too, though the menu, thankfully, is geared to the present rather than the past, and the list of beers and ciders is totally international.

Just when we thought there was nothing new on College Street, we find a menu that's divided into Salads, Snacks, Nannettes, and Scrolls. Of course, there is pasta — with a twist. Agnolotti are colourfully striped pasta pillows, plump with cheese, and tossed with olive oil, tomato, and parsley. Salads turn into productions: wild mushrooms sautéed with sun-dried tomatoes and apple in cassis, served in a radicchio cup on a bed of Belgian endive. Nannettes are oven-baked naan bread topped with any number of goodies; Scrolls are savory pastry cones filled with chicken breast, avocado, tomato, feta, and fine-herbed mayo, for example.

Originally a tiny one-room spot, they've enlarged and taken over the space next door. Still, they'll have a hard time prying me out of my favourite window seat, but at these tiny prices I can just keep ordering.

Lava Restaurant & Nightclub

507 College Street

TELEPHONE:
(416) 966-5282

CARDS:
All major credit cards

HOURS:
Dinner:
Monday to Saturday:
5:30 p.m. to 2 a.m.

(Late-night menu from
11 p.m. to midnight)

Sunday:
summer only
(call ahead)

Ask Mom or Dad about the late sixties and they may seem a little vague. It's a popular belief that if you lived through those times, you don't remember a darned thing.

That's why people of a certain vintage who walk into Lava for the first time have a feeling they've been here before. Undulating lava lamps, a stage at the rear where a band will later perform, perforated metal fixtures that send tiny beams of light over the room, and the genuine Naugahyde banquettes. While the room is steeped in funky memorabilia, the menu is crisply avant-garde. The folks who own the Rivoli and the Queen Mother have brought sushi to College Street.

Nigiri sushi comes on a slab of granite: larger than average yellowtail, salmon, arctic char, and mackerel. The drama of red lacquered chopsticks. Moving right along in Asia, velvety curried lentil soup is sweet with the taste of coconut; the portobello mushroom and red-pepper satay is skewered on branches of fresh rosemary. A sense of style, colour, and composition is expressed in a bamboo steamer dish: inside, a huge banana leaf has been folded like a turban and pinned with a large wooden skewer. Open it, and the perfume of shrimp, leek, and coconut curry on fragrant basmati rice fills the air.

After 9:30 p.m. the band comes in. The 45-seat patio offers a great view of the neighbouring garages. But who cares? You want view, go to Ontario Place.

The Midtown

552 College Street (west of Euclid)

TELEPHONE:
(416) 920-4533

CARDS:
Visa, MC

HOURS:
Every day:
noon to 2 a.m.

OTHER LOCATION:
The Midtown West
556 College Street
(416) 966-6952

The blue paint had hardly dried, there was not even a sign yet, but by 9 p.m. it was standing room only. Good news travels fast. The bare brick rooms are given character by tall benjaminas in pots and architectural improvisation. In the rear, serious-looking players hunch over the six billiard tables. The stools around the midsection of the green-stained wood bar fill up first, since this is where the chef prepares all his delicious tapas dishes: dark and crunchy tamari almonds, cold marinated mussels, bunches of dewy green grapes with wedges of pungent blue cheese, a luscious Italian sausage cut into chunks and swimming in a sauce of red peppers, a curry of cauliflower and chickpeas with top notes of coconut and cumin, slices of grilled steak splashed with tamari and ginger sauce.

The chef swirls and swivels, also preparing cold sandwiches, such as Brie with roasted red peppers, eggplant, lettuce, arugula, and olive paste between two pieces of extra-fresh bread, and grilled sandwiches such as smoked ham and Swiss cheese. Today's dinner special is a heaping bowl of seafood chowder, tomato-based, thick with scallops, shrimp, and mussels. This was the prototype bistro for the nineties.

Oasis

294 College Street (west of Spadina)

TELEPHONE:
(416) 975-0845

CARDS:
None; cash only

HOURS:
Monday to Friday:
Lunch:
11:30 a.m. to 4:30 p.m.

Dinner:
5 p.m. to midnight

Saturday:
5 p.m. to 2 a.m.

Sunday:
6 p.m. to 11 p.m.

Optimism, imagination, bravado, and a lot of love make a strong statement in this area of the city, which could well be called grunge central. Apricot-cream walls glow with murals depicting mythic desert oases of blue water, bright flowers, swimmers, dancers, and placid wild beasts. Behind the cashier, a rainbow displays its hues. Every varnished wood table offers a comfortable chair or banquette.

The personality of owner/chef Francesca Phillimore is evident. She wants everyone to be happy. And so her dinner menu offers 31 delicious small dishes at delicious small prices. Couscous is plump with fresh apricots and mint; ground-beef meatballs glisten in a tangy glaze; Greek salad is superb; chili chickpeas, jalapeño vegetable stew, and spicy chicken kebabs have all been seasoned with her canny hand to delight rather than destroy. There is no hustle. Service is gentle and patient as we ask for explanations. What are sweet-and-sour onions? What is spinach feta borek? Tasty tidbits, all. Friday nights, they open the back room for "original and intimate entertainment for the millennially challenged." To me, this says: If life is getting you down, come to the Oasis.

The Orbit Room

580-A College Street

TELEPHONE:
(416) 535-0613

CARDS:
All major credit cards

HOURS:
Monday and Tuesday:
9 p.m. to 2 a.m.

Wednesday:
7:30 p.m. to 2 a.m.

Thursday to Saturday:
7 p.m. to 2 a.m.

Sunday:
8:30 p.m. to 2 a.m.

(Kitchen closes at
11 p.m.)

It's one flight of stairs up to the Orbit Room. After 9 p.m. be prepared for an aggressive demand for a cash cover charge ($3 to $5 per person) — for the band — before you step into the room.

We have a choice of seating: at the bar area or in the navy blue velvet cocoon section with tables. The menu is to the point: 16 small items priced from $4.50 to $12.95. Caesar salad drowns perfectly good romaine and croutons in a swamp of mayo/mustard — but some people love it that way. An arrangement of lovely oyster mushrooms "orbits" around corn-on-the-cob that sports a plastic holder. Drizzles of spicy red-pepper purée and melting goat cheese add tasty frills. At 10-ish, a good-looking house band, The Dexters, start their set of sixties R&B. Since conversation is impossible now, we just enjoy the kitchen's Pacific Rim renditions. A banana leaf envelopes a filet of salmon that's been seasoned with ginger, partnered with Asian greens and a hill of spicy sticky rice, served right in the bamboo steamer. And the seared tuna is divine: a filet has been dredged with cracked black peppercorns, seared medium, sliced, and then served with a scattering of baby lettuce leaves, capped by pink ginger arranged as a rose and splashes of wasabi mayo. Big on sound, big on flavour — a small price to pay.

Sottovoce

595 College Street (at Clinton)

TELEPHONE:
(416) 536-4564

CARDS:
All major credit cards

HOURS:
Monday to Thursday:
5 p.m. to midnight

Friday and Saturday:
5 p.m. to 2 a.m.

Sunday:
summer only

A sleek wine bar stands on the corner. It's part of the new-generation "revolution" that's claimed the streets of Little Italy. Sottovoce had the benefit of a top design team who worked on a less-than-modest budget and came up with a look of restrained swank. There's lots of standing room around the red Formica bar and a classic oval table, the design repeated in an oval wall mirror.

Sottovoce translates as "in a soft voice," and speak softly the place does. In fact, four of us seated at a corner table one evening were surprised to see our waiter slip quietly through the side door, carrying our food order. The place is just too cool to have a kitchen. The cooking, apparently, is done at Trattoria Giancarlo, the restaurant next door. But this does not in any way mar the quality of our light supper. Savoury crostini with goat cheese, a platter of antipasto laden with cheeses, meats, those tiny black olives that we can never get enough of, air-dried beef, and prosciutto. Panini and simple pastas. A grilled sausage is flamed with alcohol for a bit of drama with our Cabernet. When the hour is late and the crush is great, when the music is played *a gran voce*, so you can't hear yourself give an intelligent answer, the service gets a bit harried. But who cares? Most evenings, you'll be chic to chic with great hair, casually perfect poses, designer duds, elegant smokers, politically correct makeup, and an ambience lifted straight out of a European film. A wine bar for the times.

Ted's Wrecking Yard

549 College Street

TELEPHONE:
(416) 928-5012

CARDS:
All major credit cards

HOURS:
Every day:
11 a.m. to 2 a.m.

SPERICOLATA is painted across the top of the inner doorway of this faux Mediterranean ruin. A plaster gargoyle adds mystery. Juxtaposed with all this are two computer terminals where, for $10 an hour, you can hook up to the Internet and surf the world. And on Saturday and Sunday nights, there are live bands that draw their own following. Is this a café with live bands? A bar that serves food? It's too loud for conversation, that's certain. There's something interesting brewing here, but I can't find the focus. Anyway, who cares? The crowd is young, noisy, and fun, and the Italian sandwiches look great.

Pizza is medium size, with pesto, sun-dried tomatoes, and mozzarella on a soft, thin crust. A great sandwich is garlic-roasted zucchini with goat cheese, tomato, and parsley, sprinkled with olive oil on good Italian bread. The salad of Belgian endive, yellow peppers, tomato, watercress, and pine nuts with mint vinaigrette is far from ho-hum. Later on, when a guy walks in with a huge dog on a leash, it seems perfectly natural. Not a place for a three-course meal, not a restaurant per se, this place is for grazing, surfing, and hanging out.

Ferro

769 St. Clair Avenue West

TELEPHONE:
(416) 654-9119

CARDS:
All major credit cards

HOURS:
Monday to Thursday:
11 a.m. to 1 a.m.

Friday and Saturday:
11 a.m. to 2 a.m.

Sunday:
5 p.m. to 1 a.m.

Ferro means iron in Italian, and it's everywhere: wine bottles displayed in a wrought-iron rack, steel tables embraced by curved iron chairs, and the front patio, a prime nosh spot in summer, boasts sculptured iron banquettes.

The guys who created this restaurant in a space that previously served as a pool hall (you can still shoot a few games in the rear) know that what's good and what's fresh sells. Meat-Eaters Salad, for example — char-grilled steak set on ripe tomato, onions, marinated peppers, and puckish leaves of arugula — satisfies on many levels. A big white bowlful of grilled chicken tossed with broccoli and fusilli has charm. Pasta and risotto dishes change daily. And the thin-crust 12-in. pizzas come as you like them. My pal always goes for the hamburger P.P.C. style ("pre portion control") with the works. That means a chewy Portuguese bun, braised onions, marinated peppers, grilled mushrooms, and other goodies.

Four distinct neighbourhoods converge here at Christie and St. Clair. The city archives are rich with stories about this once blue-collar area — some heart-warming, some bone-chilling. Never mind, today, it's the right place to eat well.

Filippo's Gourmet Pizza

744 St. Clair Avenue West

TELEPHONE:
(416) 658-0568

CARDS:
All major credit cards

HOURS:
Sunday to Wednesday:
5 p.m. to 10 p.m.

Thursday to Saturday:
5 p.m. to 11:30 p.m.

(Stays open one hour
later in the summer)

Closed Monday

"Life is like a pizza — the more you put in, the richer it gets." So goes the motto written on a slab of black slate shaped like the boot of Italy that hangs on the wall. What about the pizza here? Each pie is made to order and baked in a big oven till the edges char and the cheeses melt.

It's impossible not to pause at the wooden table filled with gorgeous antipasti: giant olives and polenta, green beans, potatoes and sautéed onion, grilled eggplant, charred peppers, and more. Come summer, the spacious, covered patio is the place we like to make a meal of a little of everything. A plateful of this antipasto is a thing of beauty.

The blackboard lists soups, pizzas, and risotto specials. Nice to see that the crisp Caesar salad is served at the table, family-style, from one large bowl. And house wine is poured from Italian pottery chicken decanters. You've got to have a sense of humour in this business.

So what kind of oven did Filippo Di Natale choose to bake his gourmet pizza? "The oven is gas," he says, pounding his chest, "but I am electric!"

Julie's

202 Dovercourt Road

TELEPHONE:
(416) 532-7397

CARDS:
None; cash only

HOURS:
Winter:
Tuesday to Sunday:
6 p.m. to 11 p.m.

(Drinks until midnight
or later)

Summer:
Tuesday to Friday:
6 p.m. to 11 p.m.

Saturday and Sunday:
11:30 a.m. to 11 p.m.

Closed Monday

Yes, there really is a Julie, and once upon a time, this 28-seat restaurant was her grocery store. Now the Cuban home cooking of her son-in-law Jesus draws a clientele from the close-knit neighbourhood and beyond. They come for the Ceviche, little chunks of raw fresh fish "cooked," or actually marinated, in fresh lime juice and herbs; and the Tostones (deep-fried plantain chips) and fresh salsa. Potato and chickpea stew is surprisingly delicious and filling. Some people love Yucca in a mojo (sauce) of garlic, onion, citrus, and olive oil; as for me, I'll dip up the sauce without the starchy tuber.

Main courses are traditional. You won't get fancy delivery, but you will get delicious flavour. Arroz con Pollo, for example, is saffron rice topped with chicken breasts marinated in lime juice and garlic. Picadilo is meat hash with hot and sweet peppers, raisins, almonds, and nubbins of veggies. You won't find these dishes at the Ritz.

Weekend nights, the tiny place is jammed with homesick Cubanos who come to bliss out on live Cuban music.

Mezzetta Café Restaurant

681 St. Clair Avenue West (at Christie)

TELEPHONE:
(416) 658-5687

CARDS:
All major credit cards

HOURS:
Lunch:
Tuesday to Friday:
noon to 2:30 p.m.

Dinner:
Tuesday to Sunday:
5 p.m. to 11 p.m.

Closed Monday

Wednesday nights, Yossi wears a bow tie. That's when jazz musicians like Jane Bunnett and Brian Katz thrill a polite, packed house who've paid a minuscule cover. Mezzetta, which roughly translates into "small portions of tasty food," is Yossi's dream come true, a super-casual snug enclave with rec-room décor, serving traditional Middle Eastern dishes. Combos vary: for example, meat kebabs, garden salad, hummus or tahini, and coffee, tea, or soft drinks. Or choose ten hot and cold dishes from a vast and yummy selection that includes hummus, baba ghanouj, Moroccan carrots, sautéed mushrooms, cucumbers in yogurt, Persian rice, lamb or chicken shish-sticks, falafel, vegetable bourekas, rice, and meat-stuffed vine leaves. Scoop it all up with hunks of warm pita. Servers understand our happy dilemma and help with choices. Unhurried, unharried cuisine to schmooze by. Relax with a glass of Turkish coffee and a bowl of pistachios, sunflower and pumpkin seeds, or cookies stuffed with dates and nuts. Reminds me of cozy jazz haunts in Amsterdam, Israel, Cypress, and New York.

Pizza Banfi

333-B Lonsdale Road (at Spadina)

TELEPHONE:
(416) 322-5231

CARDS:
All major credit cards

HOURS:
Lunch:
Monday to Saturday:
noon to 2:30 p.m.

Dinner:
Monday to Saturday:
5:30 p.m. to 11 p.m.

Sunday:
5:30 p.m. to 10:30 p.m.

Italian charm runs rampant at Banfi. If the food wasn't so good, the place could run on "feel good" alone. The action starts right at 5:30 p.m., when people are drawn from Forest Hill like moths to a flame by big bowls of homemade pasta — gnocchi with pink sauce, fettuccine with fresh tomato and basil sauce, penne with Gorgonzola; by steaming homemade soup — pastina in brodo, minestrone; by the addictive, crispy, thin-crusted pizza slathered with tomato sauce and a dazzling array of toppings; and by luscious Italian cake and layered café latte.

It's all prepared by a trio of handsome chefs behind the counter. By 7 p.m. the 35-seat room has been turned over to the second seating — those who have been waiting patiently at the bar, sipping good Italian wine, nibbling on spicy olives, and eyeing the vast antipasto counter. By 9 p.m. the third wave has been seated, and still people come piling in. The owner treats all customers, old and new, in the same way: with affection, sincerity, and the promise of a table. Very soon.

Savorie

390 Spadina Road

TELEPHONE:
(416) 485-3553

CARDS:
All major credit cards

HOURS:
Lunch:
Monday to Saturday:
noon to 3 p.m.

Dinner:
Monday to Saturday:
5:30 p.m. to 11 p.m.

Closed Sunday

This modern corner bistro is the offspring of twin brothers, Tony and Martino Genua, whose family owns the grocery across the street, a favourite shopping stop for Forest Hillaries.

Tony can read the mind of any hungry or thirsty customer by his sheer desire to please. Uncertain about water or wine? He suggests a long, cool one: orange juice, cranberry juice, and soda. Perfect.

Summers, the street-side patio beckons. Winters, the cozy bar or the attractive wood-panelled dining room offers solace. Appetizers like salmon carpaccio, arrayed with capers and red onion, and salads that amaze with their virtuous freshness.

There are always pasta specials, light or hearty. Orecchiette Calabrese, for example, is a luscious pasta dish plump with rapini and sausage in a spicy garlic and olive oil sauce. When we choose Penne Alla Contadina with grilled chicken, roasted red peppers, and leeks, Tony senses my hesitancy when it comes to tomato cream sauce, and he recommends a white wine, olive oil, and garlic sauce instead. And that's the way it is.

"Thursdays," says Tony, "we always have rabbit on the menu, a different way each week." And who makes that? "My mom," he replies. There goes my Thursday night bowling.

The Village Idiot

392 1/2 Spadina Road (north of St. Clair)

TELEPHONE:
(416) 488-8987

CARDS:
All major credit cards

HOURS:
Monday to Thursday:
Lunch:
noon to 3 p.m.

Dinner:
5 p.m. to 10 p.m.

Friday and Saturday:
11 a.m. to midnight

Sunday:
11 a.m. to 10 p.m.

It's not commonplace to find taxidermy in a restaurant. But then, The Village Idiot is far from a commonplace restaurant. Stuffed peacocks perch on balustrades in the storefront windows. Walls are a muralist's vision of high realism and fantasy: bricks and climbing ivy combine with the kind of tropical panorama usually seen on the sides of black vans.

The clientele is eclectic. But most evenings, a network of the neighbourhood youth have made it their home away from home. And why not? The food is delicious. Bruschetta is four slices of tomato-piled, buttery garlic toasts. A whole grilled chicken breast on a platter high with greens makes a startlingly pleasing salad. And to the kitchen's credit, the char-grilled Idiot Burger comes with this same green salad and lots of condiments. Linguine with pesto is enhanced with seasoned diced tomato and goat cheese. Though homemade, desserts are not quite good enough. Still, go. Everything else will claim your appetite.

Allen's

143 Danforth Avenue (at Broadview)

TELEPHONE:
(416) 463-3086

CARDS:
All major credit cards

HOURS:
Monday to Friday:
11:30 a.m. to 2 a.m.

Saturday:
11 a.m. to 2 a.m.

Sunday:
11 a.m. to 11 p.m.

(Kitchen closes at
11 p.m.)

Along the joyful rialto that is "the Danforth" there is a bastion of solid Americana: a polished wood, vintage New York saloon, complete with oak bar, pressed-tin ceiling, and short-order counter. Burgers, grilled chicken, and great pastas are served with panache. A big list of 45 imported and microbrewery beers vies for freshness with witty salads.

Owner John Maxwell, a pulse-taker of eating habits, knows that come summer, happiness means communing with nature. So he opened a secluded backyard garden to provide our summer thrills and grills. The captain of the massive old-fashioned barbecue will have you drooling over the succulent selection of lobster, prawns, steak, salmon, chicken, tuna, and sausages — all glistening with oils, herbs and spices. Eat as much as you want of the three "go-with" market salads. At a refreshingly small price, this package will win a place in your heart and match your budget.

Avli

401 Danforth Avenue

TELEPHONE:
(416) 461-9577

CARDS:
All major credit cards

HOURS:
Monday to Saturday:
noon to 3 a.m.

Sunday:
3 p.m. to midnight

Avli is like the hundreds of tavernas that dot the coastlines of Greece. White, roughly plastered walls, a few red clay pitchers on shelves and wavy outcroppings of plaster that lead the eye to the busy open kitchen at the back.

The simple one-page menu says, we are a Greek kitchen, and proud of it. Even the house wines are Greek. Fresh bread is thickly sliced and there's a decanter of Greek olive oil, fragrant with sprigs of oregano and cloves of garlic. You can almost make a meal of the traditional appetizers: dips like taramosalata, melitzanosalata, skordalia — ask for a combination. Then go for the vegetables: warm potatoes with artichoke hearts, marinated mushrooms, luscious beets with garlic, eggplant baked with onions, grilled zucchini with goat cheese.

What? You want me to order dinner now? Maybe I can handle a chicken pie with a puffy golden crust or a rabbit and pearl onion pie. Break open the crust and inhale the aromas.

A dessert of pressed yogurt with honey and fresh fruit, a cup of thick black Greek coffee, a glass of ouzo. We feel that just outside the door, there's a path down to the sea.

Café Brussel

786 Broadview Avenue (at Danforth)

TELEPHONE:
(416) 465-7363

CARDS:
All major credit cards

HOURS:
Brunch:
Saturday and Sunday:
9 a.m. to 3 p.m.

Dinner:
Tuesday to Saturday:
5 p.m. to 11 p.m.

Closed Monday

This area is Mediterranean, but the mood is pure Belgique. Midnight blue walls, navy linens, whimsical kitchen witches on broomsticks, a ceiling fan, and the clean smell of home baking provide a warm welcome. This delightful café, with its behind-the-stairs annex and pretty backyard garden, is Roger Wils's domain. There is no slapdash grill-to-table cooking here. Wils serves 100% organic meats, herbs from his own garden, and soups made from scratch. He bakes all the wonderful patisserie himself. Two enthusiastic, knowledgeable, and polite servers work the room.

With its fine-quality cooking and ridiculously low prices, Brussel is the kind of café you want to claim as your own. Traditional onion soup has depth of flavour and comes capped with toasted, nutty Emmenthal cheese. Salade Verte is a flurry of greens that fills a dinner plate and is lightly dressed with raspberry vinaigrette. It's clear that Wils likes to cook. He slow-simmers chicken for lush Poulet Waterzooi, the traditional Belgian chicken stew; leg of lamb is sautéed the Moroccan way with tomato, coriander, garlic, and raisins, and comes with couscous and vegetables; pork loin is stuffed with plums and pistachios and napped with green peppercorn sauce. A grilled rainbow trout is well-seasoned and firm-fleshed; steak and frites are a lot better than I had the last time I saw Paris. We'll be back for Sunday brunch — Belgian waffles with fresh whipped cream and berries sound divine.

Chopan Kebab House & Restaurant

798 Danforth Avenue

TELEPHONE:
(416) 778-1200

CARDS:
Visa, MC

HOURS:
Every day:
noon to 10 p.m.

International upheavals, shifting borders, and migrating peoples. How do we relate to these world affairs? With alacrity and an appetite for a historic cuisine. In Afghanistan, a landlocked country of herdsmen, meats roasted over open fires and root vegetables simmered in pots are the mainstays of the national diet. And dumplings, well known in every Old World kitchen, are part of the tradition.

A painted wall mural depicting a peaceful garden landscape dominates. Utilitarian furnishings are made comfortable by Afghan carpets that cover the floor and drape over booths. This is a rare opportunity to indulge in a cuisine usually prepared only in Afghan homes. Know too that all the meat is Halal, a humane method of butchering required by Muslim law.

Food is simple but delicious, and you can make a meal of a selection of these steamed meat-filled bundles — if they don't politely insist you try everything on the menu. Use the flat yeast bread to remove the kebabs from the skewers and spoon up some golden-brown vegetable basmati rice. Fragrant tea ends the meal.

Christina's

492 Danforth Avenue (at Logan)

TELEPHONE:
(416) 463-4418

CARDS:
All major credit cards

HOURS:
Sunday to Thursday:
10:30 a.m. to 2 a.m.

Friday and Saturday:
10:30 a.m. to 4 a.m.

For the people whose lives begin at the edge of night, a good time includes hanging around the street that never sleeps: the Danforth. Step inside the wrought-iron gateposts to Christina's patio, and if you're lucky, a bright blue or yellow table will be vacant. Friendly, outgoing staff can guide you through the vast Greek/Italian menu to the "Light Tonight" section for chicken souvlaki in a pita with fries or salad. The all-day breakfast centres on two organic eggs and all the fixings, but if you're seriously hungry, try Christina's massive mixed plate for two — lamb chops, biftekia, quails, loukaniko, and kebabs, with a large Greek salad and veggies. I like to relax here and eat with my hands, dipping chunks of warm pita into lush hummus, eggplant purée, taramosalata, and tzadziki.

If it's too cold, the inside is good too. Check out the testimonial wall of movie star photos from Mitsou to Mick Jagger and the carved slabs of black marble brought from Greece. Thursday to Saturday there is live music — bouzouki, guitar, and vocalist — and a whole lot of cruising going on.

Hayama Sushi Bar Japanese Restaurant

784 Broadview Avenue

TELEPHONE:
(416) 778-8543

CARDS:
All major credit cards

HOURS:
Tuesday to Sunday:
5 p.m. to 11 p.m.

Closed Monday

The best place to be in this tiny restaurant is at the sushi counter. Yuki-san, the sushi chef, is an artist at his craft. Not a grain of rice is out of place as he makes an inside-out California roll. Not a single bright red egg of flying-fish roe is lost in his capable hands. If I hadn't seen him making a perfect maki-zushi set with my own eyes, I wouldn't have thought it was real food.

People fill the tables in the pretty dining room, enjoying set meals that include miso soup, salad, and a main course like teriyaki or tempura. During peak hours you may need to negotiate for a reservation near the time you'd prefer to come in. Frankly, the best time to dine here and "counter-sit" is when it's not too busy. Then you can ask Yuki-san if he wouldn't mind going off-menu to create some sushi especially for you.

The Myth

417 Danforth Avenue

TELEPHONE:
(416) 461-8383

CARDS:
All major credit cards

HOURS:
Sunday to Wednesday:
5 p.m. to 1 a.m.

Thursday to Saturday:
5 p.m. to 4 a.m.

Walking a tightrope between garishness and genuine glamour, this décor pushes the bounds of good taste. But frankly, it's just the right ambience for the fifties Hercules movie or Marilyn Monroe in *Gentlemen Prefer Blondes* — myths all — that play without sound on huge suspended TV screens. The gold, hammered-copper, black, and maroon colour scheme creates a velvety intimacy in a vast space that was a theatre in a former life. Both menu and theme take a non-trad route to Greece, detouring through California.

With a no-reservations policy in effect, you may feel you'll have to wait for a table. But it soon becomes obvious that a table isn't necessary. You can perch at the bar, munch on spanakopita and calamari, or eat sandwiches filled with bresaola, Parmesan, and arugula. Or nibble crispy-crust pizzas. There are five pool tables — a couple can rack 'em and stack 'em all the while enjoying a basket of grilled focaccia, pita, and Calabrese bread with a combination platter of zippy Mediterranean dips. But please, don't drop crumbs on the green felt tables. Grazing food aside, the kitchen does nicely with grilled lamb chops and colossal prawns sold by the piece. Those who live by night will be happy to know that Myth is open until the crack of dawn on the weekends.

Ouzeri

500-A Danforth Avenue (at Logan)

TELEPHONE:
(416) 778-0500

CARDS:
All major credit cards

HOURS:
Monday, Wednesday
and Thursday:
11:30 a.m. to midnight

Tuesday:
11:30 a.m. to 3 a.m.
(Greek party night)

Friday and Saturday:
11:30 a.m. to 1 a.m.

Sunday:
11:30 a.m. to 11 p.m.

Ouzeri is still the coolest spot on the hot, hot Danforth. Even though its gadabout culinary creator is no longer in the picture, his Greek dips of taramosalata, tzadziki, hummus, and skordalia — a fluffy whip of potato and garlic — all scooped up with chunks of warm homemade pita, are potent as neon.

Come summer, Ouzeri becomes even more of a favourite. Grazers find fertile pasture and vegetarians find Nirvana on this menu. The appetizer list alone offers 15 selections without meat. Also, there's Yemista Politika, a huge grilled green pepper stuffed with rice, pine nuts, onions, raisins, and celery, astride a bed of grape leaves drenched with lemon and olive oil. For carnivores, there's a dish of big chunks of grilled lamb in feta sauce with lots of fresh green garnish. Alas, Saganaki is not served flaming in its frying pan amid shouts of "Opa!" "It's too crowded in here for that!" shouts our waiter above the bouzouki music that bounces off the painted tiles. Don't come here if you have a fear of intimacy: tables are very close together. But the atmosphere is wonderfully relaxing.

Le Commensal Fine Vegetarian Cuisine

655 Bay Street (at Elm)

TELEPHONE:
(416) 596-9364

CARDS:
All major credit cards

HOURS:
Monday to Friday:
11:30 a.m. to 10 p.m.

Saturday and Sunday:
noon to 10 p.m.

The name means "table-mate" *en français*, and the restaurant is one of a privately owned Montreal chain. They say "non" to meat and fish, artificial colouring, flavouring, and additives, and "oui" to a grand, vegetarian buffet.

Strolling along the 100-item, self-serve cafeteria and filling my plate with bits of food described as to their vegetarian, lacto, or ovo components is an adventure. Colourful sandwich loafs and pâtés all look delicious, but what are they really made of? Tofu, seitan, and other faux food. Still, there are many positive reasons for embracing the vegetarian food style. A bowl of hearty vegetable soup and a few slices of earnestly healthy bread; a pretty salad of organic greens, flower petals, and four kinds of sprouts; crisp Chinese vegetable salad. A real find is the kasha with sweet potato, a tasty combination of nutty and sweet flavours. After all of the above, I take a main-course portion of yummy mashed potatoes.

The next step is from the food counters to the cash desk. Here, the plate is weighed and priced.

A window table along Elm Street is a terrific place to spend time with a glass of fresh juice pumped up with a hit of wheat grass. Or a dandy cup of coffee or herbal tea with a slice of fine apple pie. And since you serve yourself, there's no tipping, unless you contribute to the "tip jar" at the cash register.

Ethiopian House

4 Irwin Avenue (west of Yonge)

TELEPHONE:
(416) 923-5438

CARDS:
All major credit cards

HOURS:
Every day:
noon to midnight

Unsure which fork to use? No problem: no cutlery. In this pretty, 40-seat restaurant, a spongy pancake-like bread, injera, serves as food, fork, and sometimes plate. Never having eaten at the source, we take a tip from the menu and order Bayaaynatu (literally, "combination"), which comes with or without meat, as you prefer. Ours is a variety of small servings of highly seasoned chickpeas and mixed vegetables (stringbeans, carrots, tomatoes), beef sautéed with vegetables and awaze (a spice mixture), kale, and lentils.

The culture of Ethiopia is showcased along with the food. A server in traditional embroidered dress brings a huge enamel pan, almost the size of the table, covered by a bonnet woven of brightly coloured reeds. Remove the bonnet to reveal injera heaped with mounds of spicy vegetables and even spicier meats. We break off pieces of injera and go around the plate pinching up bits of food. The flavours are unusual — but spicily satisfying. Hints of dry red pepper, cardamom, cloves, ginger, fenugreek, and other exotics have seasoned Ethiopian food for centuries. The spice mixtures that define this cuisine are called berbere, awaze, and mitmita. Mead (a honey wine), Tusker Lager, and South African wines complement the menu, and a dramatic painted wall mural gives a sense of the country.

Just Desserts

555 Yonge Street (at Wellesley)

TELEPHONE:
(416) 963-8089

CARDS:
All major credit cards

HOURS:
Sunday to Thursday:
10:30 a.m. to 1 a.m.

Friday and Saturday:
10:30 a.m. to 3 a.m.

OTHER LOCATIONS:
1985 Queen Street East
(416) 693-1288

1198 St. Clair Avenue
West
(416) 658-0078

4909 Yonge Street
(416) 222-5748

1830 The Queensway
(416) 622-2885

"Too much of a good thing is wonderful!" I'm for that. Especially when the good things are 21 different kinds of extraordinary, homemade, mouth-watering cakes; ten different deep-dish pies; eight of the lushest, highest cheesecakes you've ever laid eyes on; and a delectable assortment of cookies and tarts. As my Mama once said, "If you looked at a man like you look at a piece of cake, you'd have been married long ago."

But there's more to this café than just a pretty cake. There's Hollywood's favourite salad, a crisp Caesar capped with grilled chicken breast. If you yearn for some Italian comfort food, try multi-layered meat or veggie lasagna. The house special, Rotolo, will make your day — it's a soft dough, filled with grilled chicken, mushroom, pepper, and onion, baked in the oven and smothered with marinara sauce. For folks who like to tipple with their tiramisu, there's a full bar. And there's a great-looking pool table. After grappling with a big chunk of chocolate cake, some bending and stretching over a cue is a good thing.

From the day the doors opened — and they're open long hours — there has been a lineup to get into these places. Could be because everything that's served is absolutely fresh and delicious. As Marie Antoinette recommended, "Let them eat cake!"

Mammina's

6 Wellesley Street West

TELEPHONE:
(416) 967-7199

CARDS:
All major credit cards

HOURS:
Lunch:
Tuesday to Friday:
11 a.m. to 2 p.m.

Dinner:
Tuesday to Saturday:
5 p.m. to 10 p.m.

Closed Sunday
and Monday

Paulo and Davide Valentini, a couple of sentimental guys from Calabria, opened this little gem of a restaurant and called it Mammina's, the name they called their beloved grandmother. So right away we know the cooking will be done as it should be. From the simple — Linguine al Pesto, with snippets of basil leaves, a sprinkle of pine nuts, and the perfume of garlic and olive oil — to the complex — Linguine Mammina, with juicy pieces of chicken, green peppercorns, cream, and a hint of licorice from a splash of Pernod. Vitello Lombardo is a triumph with its sauce of peppers, mushrooms, tomato, addictive wine-soaked olives, and a generous side of spaghetti. Herb-touched steamed mussels in a garlic tomato sauce makes a fine beginning.

Crisp-white ladder-back chairs add sparkle to a plain but neat two-tiered room. And it's surprisingly peaceful considering its location on a chrome-to-chrome thoroughfare. With over ten years of serving grateful Italophiles, from the high and flighty jet-setting film stars who stay at the nearby Sutton Place Hotel to the dedicated local clientele, Mammina would be proud.

Okonomi House

23 Charles Street West

TELEPHONE:
(416) 925-6176

CARDS:
Visa, MC

HOURS:
Every day:
11 a.m. to 10 p.m.

Okonomiyaki is the newest Japanese cuisine to hit the West. It's only been around for about a hundred years. Let's not look at it as "fast food," since most Japanese food falls into that category. Okonomiyaki is a cross between Canadian flapjacks and a French omelette — and like these, it's made to order.

First, choose your favourite fillings: seafood, vegetable, bacon, or whatever. The griddler begins cooking and seasoning the fillings at once. Meanwhile, you can nibble on an array of reasonably priced appetizers. When the filling is cooked, the griddler pours a thick pancake-like batter over top and lets it all cook together into a saucer-sized flapjack. Flip, he turns it over and lets it sizzle and crisp on the other side. In Japan, they smear a kind of mayonnaise over top and then make a design with zippy steak sauce. This is one dish that has crossed the Pacific intact.

Add a few side dishes like sunomono, noodle soup, or a whole yakiniku dinner. There's even beef, salmon, or tofu teriyaki. In this tiny midtown space, the value is teri-iffic.

Rugantino

30 Charles Street West

TELEPHONE:
(416) 922-3923

CARDS:
All major credit cards

HOURS:
Lunch:
Monday to Friday:
11:30 p.m. to 2:30 p.m.

Dinner:
Monday to Saturday:
5 p.m. to 10:30 p.m.

Closed Sunday

Sometimes we need a break from new eateries that serve Cal–Ital, Cal–Greek, Cal–Conti, and Cal–Cal. What we long for is traditional Ital–Ital in a restaurant that has been around for a long time and has paid its dues. John Varrecchia has owned Rugantino for 30 years, and very little has changed during his long reign. The commercial wood–panelled walls, patterned tile floor, and comfortable chairs do not hint at fancy decorating. But no one's complaining, they're here for the food — and the complimentary antipasto of marinated vegetables, grassini, soft bread, and a ramekin of chicken liver pâté.

John cooks best what he knows best: eggplant parmigiana, for example, is a layering of thinly sliced eggplant, tomato sauce, and mozzarella, baked slowly 'til it's tender and bubbly; broad slabs of spinach pasta are used to create a handsome, old-fashioned lasagna; ricotta cheese and spinach manicotti and stuffed cannelloni are still made in the same way he learned to make them years ago as a boy in Campagna. The daily specials are a steal. For example, chicken cacciatore with spaghetti, soup or salad, and coffee is just over $10.

The garnish is a sprig of domestic curly parsley placed on a piece of flat-leaf Italian parsley — Can–Ital. "My customers are my family," he says, "and I like to look after them."

7 West Café

7 Charles Street West

TELEPHONE:
(416) 928-9041

CARDS:
All major credit cards

HOURS:
Always open

Sitting at a small table by the window on the second floor, I feel like I have been sucked into my TV set. I am an extra in a TV show called "7 West Café." The casting is perfect: musclemen in undershirts, strong-jawed young women ... except for a smattering of mature faces, most are under 30. People with good haircuts and good bones. No one looks dangerous. An invisible director has said, "Action!" Everyone is animated, table-hopping, talking, smoking, eating, running up and down the stairs to the third floor, where there is a pool table and a roof garden patio.

Through all this, the owners stay calm, beautiful, and don't let anyone see them sweat. These three young women are living a life that appears glamorous but is really hard work. They've converted a narrow row house into a haven for the hip and hungry. Their café never closes and has a one-page menu that they've all mastered. Surprising how many people hunger for pasta primavera, vegetarian chili, or a bagel melt at 3 a.m. And everything comes with green salad. Every item is homemade. Soups like Moroccan lentil, carrot, and potato-leek are delicious. Pasta salad is fresh and yummy, and dinner-size sandwiches (smoked turkey, hot prosciutto fritté) are huge. On the main floor, check out the chic antipasto/wine bar.

Spadina Garden

114 Dundas Street West

TELEPHONE:
(416) 977-3413/4

CARDS:
All major credit cards

HOURS:
Monday to Thursday:
11:30 a.m. to 9:45 p.m.

Friday and Saturday:
11:30 a.m. to 10:45 p.m.

Sunday:
4 p.m. to 9:45 p.m.

(Free delivery 5 p.m.
to 9 p.m. for orders
over $20)

An embarrassment of riches — that's what we've got here. The Chen family has owned Spadina Garden for over a decade, and their dishes are Toronto classics. Barbecued honey-garlic spareribs and crisp spring rolls as appetizers. The table agrees: good, yummy, and just a shade greasy — but hey, if we wanted non-greasy, we could go for Triple Delight bean curd soup.

The room itself is calm, with standard-issue black lacquer high-back chairs and bright red paper lanterns hanging from the ceiling. This is Szechuan food from the mountains, not a cuisine of fresh fish. So there is no tank of finny creatures to peruse. But there are 211 searing dishes to choose from: orange beef, for example, a dark, saucy dish; Szechuan chicken, slices of white chicken meat and vegetables in a radiant red chili seasoning. Beef with black mushrooms and oyster sauce gets no complaints from me. A round of applause goes to General Tso's chicken. These deep-fried clusters of chicken in a bright red sauce are the first to disappear off the plate.

I'm happy with my perfumed tea and the cryptic message in my fortune cookie: "Many possibilities are open to you — work a little harder." Does that mean I should eat more?

Spring Roll on Yonge

687 Yonge Street

TELEPHONE:
(416) 972-7655

CARDS:
Visa, MC

HOURS:
Every day:
11:30 a.m. to 11 p.m.

(Free delivery 4 p.m.
to 11 p.m. for orders
over $15)

The egg roll is dead, done in by its crusty cousin, the spring roll. We've embraced this import from Southeast Asia with a fervour once reserved for domestic fast foods, like hot and spicy wings or a pizza slice. Which of the eight spring rolls to choose? The "house" roll filled with half a dozen crisp veggies, ground chicken, and tiger shrimp; cold shrimp rolls, the yummy Filipino-style cold shrimp rolls with shrimp, mango, and vermicelli; cold vegetable spring rolls? When we can't decide, we let them do it and ask for a Spring Roll Platter. It's a win/win situation.

We're on a roll. The menu takes us on a culinary sojourn through Southeast Asia. A bowl of steamy Vietnamese broth, Pho Saigon, with rare and well-done beef; on to vegetable and tofu stir-fry in Szechuan sauce, grilled teriyaki chicken breast, and a small order of vermicelli with lemon grass and roasted peanuts. The traditional fruit shakes like mango, avocado, even carrot, seem to be just the right drink with these dishes.

No reservations and a lineup at all hours confirms that this is one terrific eatery.

Mool Rae Bang-A

3 Christie Street

TELEPHONE:
(416) 534-6833

CARDS:
Visa, MC

HOURS:
Every day:
11 a.m. to 1 a.m.

To really enjoy Korean food, you must embrace kimchee. But, I must confess that these nubbins of cabbage, pickled and fermented in a brine that includes chilis, garlic, ginger, and anchovy paste, will never be appreciated by me. So, I do not come *tabula rasa* to Korean cuisine. I do, however, come with a curiosity as to what's going down in the rising tide of Korean restaurants with Hangul lettering that have sprung up on Bloor Street West.

Our server slips through the doorway of our wood-screened cubicle and the culinary adventure begins. Pungent roasted green tea and an array of Korean appetizers. These small dishes are the personal signature of the house; here, we're served seaweed salad, crisp shards of grated radish, a bowl of vinegared mung bean sprouts, a cluster of lightly steamed spinach. Awaiting the main course are a plate piled high with crisp lettuce leaves and a bowl of orange miso paste with sesame seeds and chili. Mauve bean curd Jello splashed with a sauce of soy, sesame oil, and chili pepper seems rather bland. Later, I come to appreciate its qualities. As in most Asian cuisines, all the food comes at once. Our server places a round grill on the table and arranges bulgogi, raw marinated beef, over its hot surface. The tender, flavourful beef browns and crisps quickly. Take a lettuce leaf, spread with miso paste, top with grilled beef, fold and eat. Delicious. Then the ferocious heat of the orange paste kicks in. Quick, the bean curd Jello!

The Queen of Sheba

1198 Bloor Street West (west of Dufferin)

TELEPHONE:
(416) 536-4162

CARDS:
Visa, MC

HOURS:
Every day:
11 a.m. to 11 p.m.

Ethiopian tradition says, "Break bread together and strengthen the bonds of loyalty and friendship." The Queen of Sheba is a great place to do just that.

Fiery food is seasoned with berbere, a paste of paprika, chilis, and spices, or with a more delicate spice, alechas, and is served in little mounds on injera, a porous, spongy, sourdough flatbread that comes on a tray almost the size of your table. Forget plates, forks, and knives. Break off a piece of bread, scoop up a tasty tidbit of chicken, beef, or lamb stew — or if you prefer vegetables: kale and potato or lentil and onions — and a cluster of greens. The House Platter for two gives a good sampling of everything.

Non-intimidating, almost romantic ambience, with a varied and loyal clientele. Mirrors reflect flickering candles. A smoky goblet of frankincense and a blackened pot of thick Turkish-like coffee, fitted into its own brass and wood table, complete this dining adventure.

Ristorante Roma

1090 Bloor Street West (at Dufferin)

TELEPHONE:
(416) 531-4000

CARDS:
All major credit cards

HOURS:
Monday to Friday:
10 a.m. to 4 a.m.

Saturday and Sunday:
4 p.m. to 4 a.m.

We sometimes long for the good old days. Old-fashioned thick-crust pizza, a big plate of spaghetti with meat sauce, really good tiramisu. In the Bloorcourt area, there is Roma, a friendly neighbourhood eatery. They offer the full menu until the wee hours of the morning, seven days a week. Do people really want to eat in the middle of the night? You bet! There's everything you ever hungered for in pizza, traditional or gourmet, and salads that include Caesar, Greek, or Roma, with lettuce, avocado, green beans, and sun-dried tomatoes. Veal sandwiches like Mama used to make. Overstuffed lasagna and cannelloni. A platter of Risotto Frutti de Mare — tomato-sauced rice generously tossed with shrimp, squid, and mussels — is almost too much to eat.

Choose a seat close to the window in the easygoing bar section up front, or one in the rear at a white-clothed table. The menu is the same. And if you can't get out and need a fresh seafood panzerotto fix, or crave a Roma Deluxe pizza with pepperoni, mushrooms, green peppers, bacon, onions, and olives — just call. On any order over $9, they deliver. Free.

Sejong Japanese/ Korean Restaurant

658 Bloor Street West

TELEPHONE:
(416) 535-5918,
(416) 537-5296

CARDS:
All major credit cards

HOURS:
Every day:
11:30 a.m. to 1 a.m.

(Kitchen closes at midnight)

On the days you feel basta with pasta, dim-sum-ed up to here and totally confused about fusion, investigate the United Nations of culinary experience around Bloor and Christie.

How do we know exactly what to order? Menus show clear colour photos of each dish, and it's reassuring, later, to see that what we get looks exactly like its picture. Almost at once, large ceramic mugs of barley tea appear, and the moment we place our order, a seven-plate parade of bright namul (antipasto) and a kimchee pancake on a sizzling iron plate. Our chopsticks fly — and there's not a tired-looking dish in the bunch.

Service is so brisk, we hardly make a dent in our miso soup, when a wicker basket of delectable tempura arrives. Feathery crisp-fried shrimp, sweet potatoes, peppers, and zucchini with a bowl of dipping sauce. And here's our sliced marinated beef and a table cooker. Too fast, too fast. We've only ordered two main courses, and yet there seems to be too much food. As in most Asian cuisines, all the food is brought at once.

In midwinter, when you're blue with cold, the red-hot flavours in Korean cuisine will blast open those blocked sinuses, perk up flagging taste buds, and make you wonder where this stuff has been all your life.

Autogrill

495 Eglinton Avenue West

TELEPHONE:
(416) 489-0961

CARDS:
All major credit cards

HOURS:
Monday to Wednesday:
11 a.m. to 10 p.m.

Thursday to Sunday:
11 a.m. to 11 p.m.

Drive along the autostradas of Italy, from Rome to Milan, for example, turn off at a rest spot, and you'll find an Autogrill rather than McDonald's or Pizza Hut.

This modern, slick design features a mirrored ceiling, a counter of savoury take-outs, and a brilliant menu of salads and pastas. And where else but on Eglinton could you get a toasted bagel and Nutella with a steaming latte macchiato? Italian sandwiches all come with a side house salad; the combinations, such as prosciutto, bocconcini, roasted peppers, and tomatoes, are delectable.

From the section called Starta da Meal there are inventive salads like spinach with diced oranges, goat cheese, and crushed walnuts slicked with mango vinaigrette, or grilled portobello mushrooms with organic greens. On to Using da Noodle: the kitchen goes out of its way to keep us pointed in a healthy direction with soya spaghetti tossed with Italian fennel sausage, peppers, and garlic, or whole-wheat penne primavera. But the pasta that brings out the kid in me is multicoloured vegetable wagon wheels tossed with peppers, sun-dried tomatoes, and green onion in a light tomato sauce. Order your pasta in a Zuppiera (a huge Italian ceramic basin that serves five) and you'll be in the heaven reserved for pastaholics.

And here's what they see as the Canadase pizza: roasted garlic, black forest ham, onions, and chicken. Take a bite, and you'll stand up and salute the flag.

Jerusalem Restaurant

955 Eglinton Avenue West (west of Bathurst)

TELEPHONE:
(416) 783-6494

CARDS:
All major credit cards

HOURS:
Monday to Friday:
11:30 a.m. to 11 p.m.

Saturday:
noon to 11:30 p.m.

Sunday:
noon to 9:30 p.m.

OTHER LOCATION:
125 Raval Road
(northeast corner of
Finch & Leslie)
(416) 490-7888

When the Jerusalem opened on Eglinton in 1971, it brought Middle Eastern hummus and tahini to a bagels–and–lox neighbourhood. Now that the partners have branched out, the menu has had a few alterations, but basically, little has changed. Two almost identical rooms are usually filled at dinner with a loyal neighbourhood crowd, who swear by the salads and dips.

Service is perfunctory. The waiter is here to serve, not to "make" your evening. You can go the appetizers–only route. Hummus circles a small mound of chopped fried meat and roasted pine nuts or comes topped with hot fava beans. A whole eggplant is thickly sliced, spiked with garlic, and fried. Sliced tomatoes are sautéed in a garlicky hot pepper and tomato sauce. A surprise is the tabbouleh — you'd need a magnifying glass to find the cracked wheat; it's mostly minced parsley. Falafel come six to an order. So now, break off a pocket of pita bread and fill it with a taste of each dish. Some good, eh? You can also take the entrée route. A whole fresh sea bass is fried to crunchy goodness and comes with a dish of tahini. They charcoal-broil a marinated chicken breast and bring it with rice, salad, pickles, and pita — it's a good deal. Turkish coffee, perfumed with rosewater and cardamom, is interesting — which is much more than can be said for the baklava.

Pizza Pazza

1007 Eglinton Avenue West (west of Bathurst)

TELEPHONE:
(416) 785-8784

CARDS:
All major credit cards

HOURS:
Tuesday to Thursday:
5:30 p.m. to 11 p.m.

Friday and Saturday:
5:30 p.m. to midnight

Sunday:
5:30 p.m. to 11 p.m.

Closed Monday

Put Pizza Pazza on your hotline. What makes it so special? Fruitwood. The *pizzaoli* (that's the guy who makes the pizza) keeps his wood-burning clay oven all fired up from lunch 'til closing every day. He pushes the small logs to the back and the sides, and bakes the pizza on slabs, just until the edges are charred and blistered. The aroma of the wood adds a distinctive edge — as if these 10-in. thin-crust pizzas didn't have flavour enough! Here are some favourites from the list of over 20. Piu Pazza Ancora: tomato sauce, hot peppers, shrimp, spicy capicolla, Parmesan, and mozzarella. La Forbice: tomato sauce, mushrooms, chicken, and Swiss cheese, served with scissors so you can cut your own sections. Lagna Lagna: white pizza with no tomato sauce, just smoked salmon, capers, onions, and mozzarella. Fru Fru: tomato sauce, porcini mushrooms, onion, smoked bacon, and mozzarella. Irresistible.

Within these cheerful muralled walls, there's a lot more than pizza. A big bowl of plump mussels in a puddle of white wine and tomato Bruschetta Cuckoo with tuna, onion, celery, and marinated fresh beans are great starters. Salads are fresh and generous. Try the Caprese with sliced tomato and bocconcini, or the Insalata Pazza with tomato, olive, cucumbers, and onions. Both arrive with extra-virgin olive oil to dip your bread into. A few pastas complete the picture. Of course, it's noisy and young and fine. And the cappuccino is divine.

Yitz's Deli

346 Eglinton Avenue West (at Avenue Road)

TELEPHONE:
(416) 487-4506

CARDS:
All major credit cards

HOURS:
Monday to Friday:
9 a.m. to 9 p.m.

Saturday and Sunday:
9:30 a.m. to 9 p.m.

You can ask Mr. Yitz anything, except why he, Mrs. Yitz, and the whole family wear red socks. Here, in the true spirit of delicatessen design, the door handles are fat salamis, the menu, a double-rye sandwich. This is the kind of casual spot where you can drop in on a "bad hair day" or come dressed to the nines. Whatever. You'll see some of the city's power brokers dining here with the family, kids sitting in booster chairs, spraying ketchup. Yitz seems to know everyone, and even first-timers are made to feel welcome.

Good chicken and matzoh ball soup, excellent roast chicken, and crackling brown lengths of kishke (if you have to ask what it is, never mind). A good bet is the dinner that includes a 14-oz. grilled chopped steak crowned by a pepperoni (a hamburger for fressers) and a slab of fabulous lemon meringue pie. And you can't lose with a quick corned beef on rye before a movie. There are a few clunkers on the menu, but hey, that's life. Personally, I've had better potato latkes, and frankly, the vegetable soup is a tad heavy on the salt. But the burlap bag of sunflower seeds near the front could bring a tear to the eye of a homesick New Yorker. It's hard to walk out of here empty-handed, especially when you pass the bake shop where the air is perfumed with the scent of bagels, challah, sinfully good cinnamon-pecan rolls, and chunky chocolate chip cookies.

EGLINTON WEST

Brasserie Bobino

4243 Dundas Street West (at Royal York Road)

TELEPHONE:
(416) 237-1457

CARDS:
All major credit cards

HOURS:
Lunch:
Monday to Friday:
11:30 a.m. to 2 p.m.

Dinner:
Every day:
5 p.m. to 10 p.m.

In either language, the fine French cooking in this little shopping plaza restaurant is superb. From France with flair, what a wonderful surprise! Cochonnailles, an assortment of pâtés, rillettes, ham and garlic sausage, a fine green salad, and some slices of French baguette are as Gallic as you'd find in the French countryside. And I thought I'd said a final *au revoir* to ballottine, a stuffed chicken leg with Dijon mustard sauce, when Italian food became the trendy cuisine. Rack of lamb is a favourite here, and when owner and hostess Irene Mercurio describes it so enthusiastically, it's an offer one cannot refuse. Veal Provençale is lighter fare, exactly the right dish when we agree that we won't leave 'til we've indulged in the decadent chocolate mousse for dessert.

The collection of French art gallery posters reminds Chef Alain Guibray of his home. Pretty marble bistro tables, sparkling ambience, and authentic flavours remind us of France as well. Except that there are no dogs under the table.

Gente

2982 Bloor Street West

TELEPHONE:
(416) 234-9433

CARDS:
All major credit cards

HOURS:
Bar:
Every day:
11 a.m. to midnight

Restaurant:
Every day:
11 a.m. to 11 p.m.

At Gente, you will find seasonal Italian cuisine, described without adjectives and cooked without guile. Pasta is served al dente with sprightly sauces. Fettuccine Fantasia is a medley of fresh vegetables and delicious pasta kissed in a rich yet light creamy sauce; ever-changing risottos are thoughtfully prepared with seasonal ingredients; and scallopini with fungi is a marriage of flavours sure to please. Who cares about the "fat police" when there is a mountain of crispy calamari with a dish of tangy salsa? Follow it with a bowl of al dente rigatoni with artichokes and fresh tomato sauce, and the drive to Etobicoke becomes delicious diversion.

This is the archetypal affluent neighbourhood restaurant — attractive ambience, good food, livable prices, cool attitude, and some of the best espresso in the city.

McNie's Lovely Grub

315 Burnhamthorpe Road

TELEPHONE:
(416) 231-6916

CARDS:
Visa

HOURS:
Tuesday to Thursday:
11:30 a.m. to 7:30 p.m.

Friday:
11:30 a.m. to 8 p.m.

Saturday and Sunday:
12:30 p.m. to 7:30 p.m.

Closed Monday

If Irn Bru runs through your veins, if marrowfat peas, Gloucester sausage, or haggis gives you a thrill, if fish and chips is something you've been missing — then head for McNie's. On a Friday, this charming Scottish restaurant will sell 800 orders of fish and chips, which adds up to 20 tons of halibut a year. Frank McNie learned the secret of making authentic fish and chips at the big station hotels in Scotland and, believe me, you won't find his match anywhere in the city! He's got more than one fish to fry, and uses a mix of three different kinds of flour and little else to fry them in.

The best part is, you don't have to float a loan for flounder or pay through the gills for plaice, and the bill for haddock or halibut will hardly dent your wallet. An order gives you two huge pieces of golden crispy batter-fried fish, or a whole flat plaice, deep-fried without batter. Chips are made from only one kind of potato, the Burbank Netted Gem, which fries up crisp and brown. Pickled onions, pickled beets, coleslaw, a jug of gravy, Frank's own sauce, and a selection of white and malt vinegars add zip. For dessert, there's June's Scottish Trifle. Great Scot! You can feed the whole clan for under $50.

The Red Devil

199 North Queen Street

TELEPHONE:
(416) 621-4555

CARDS:
All major credit cards

HOURS:
Sunday to Thursday:
11 a.m. to midnight

Friday and Saturday:
11 a.m. to 1 a.m.

OTHER LOCATION:
14 Duncan Street
(416) 598-5209

Where there's smoke, there's barbecue. And they're really smokin' at The Red Devil. Most everything on the menu has a hint of the great smoky outdoors.

The cutlery is wrapped in old-fashioned dishtowels. Unfurl and dig in. Try the Bad to the Bone Ribs or mustard-glazed, bourbon-barbecued, jalapeño-and-mango-crusted, or applewood-smoked prime ribs. Two-fisted sandwiches like hot corned beef stacked with coleslaw come with crisp fries and melted Swiss. Pasta dishes come in two sizes: lighter and full. Trust me, unless you're an Argo linebacker, a light order of spit-roasted chicken and broccoli linguine is full enough. Now don't think they've neglected their sense and sensibilities here: there's a lovely grilled vegetable and goat cheese salad and, included in the section called Big Mouth Burgers, a veggie burger that's made from scratch daily. Desserts are in the take-no-prisoners category.

This place is cool enough for the kids, hip enough for teens, hot enough for twenty-somethings, and sensitive to fatherhood — there's a change-table in the men's room.

Marché

BCE Place (at Yonge & Wellington)

TELEPHONE:
(416) 366-8986

CARDS:
All major credit cards

HOURS:
Monday to Friday:
7 a.m. to 2 a.m.

Saturday and Sunday:
9 a.m. to 2 a.m.

Mövenpick's Marché is like a potent new drug on the market. Try it once and you're hooked. You'll love introducing it to your friends too. The atmosphere, the look, the cooking stalls with dozens of different dishes are like a microcosm of Europe. Baskets are stacked everywhere. Herbs grow in pots, wine chills, fresh fruits and vegetables are piled high, an enormous bank of crushed ice holds huge, bright-eyed fish. Oysters are shucked to order. Steaks, chops, sausages, and game birds wait to be grilled. Pizza, pasta, salads quiver with freshness. And rosti (a Euro-latke of a superior breed) comes with sour cream and perhaps smoked salmon or sausages. At the bakery, they braid dough and bake loaves before your eyes. Carmelita and Café Croquant ice cream never tasted better. Sit under trees, or in any number of environments. Black leather jackets rub shoulders with black-tie socialites, young parents with babes in arms sit next to execs with briefcases. The friendly staff exudes a welcome to all.

The choices are mind-boggling. A pizza and a glass of wine, a huge bowl of fresh pasta with stir-fried veggies and fresh salmon chunks, a half-dozen Malpeques with all the fixings, Caesar or green salads with freshly sautéed chicken or ratatouille. My favourite is a spit-roasted Cornish hen with a big baked potato. Plant geraniums in your stove and say goodbye to supermarket lineups. You can't cook for less.

Masquerade Café Bar

BCE Place (at Yonge & Front)

TELEPHONE:
(416) 363-8971

CARDS:
All major credit cards

HOURS:
Monday to Wednesday:
11:30 a.m. to midnight

Thursday to Saturday:
11:30 a.m. to 1 a.m.

Take-out: 7:30 a.m. to
midnight

Closed Sunday

We step into the Fellini-esque environment of Masquerade and find that the red, yellow, blue, and green colours lift the spirit immediately. An eccentric array of upholstered sofas, chairs, and banquettes invites us to park at whatever seating arrangement strikes our fancy. The short menu does not tax our patience and the moderate prices soothe our beleaguered bankbooks. Snaking across the ceiling is a brilliant lighting fixture of hand-blown Murano glass, adding sparkle to the huge red, blue, and green enamel stoves that stand imposingly on a stage. Bowls of chunky Parmesan and marinated olives in tomato chutney welcome us at the table.

On today's specials menu (it changes daily) is one soup: delicious roasted onion with pesto croutons; one salad: exotic greens with tuna, cheese, olives, and marinated mushrooms; two antipasti: one of zesty marinated seafood, the other earthier; one risotto: saffron and porcini mushrooms; and one pasta: a divine handmade mushroom ravioli in an herb cream. Panini Famosi — sensational sandwiches on long homemade buns with scrumptious fillings — are grilled in Italian sandwich presses. Bresaola, Brie, and arugula; Italian smoked speck and Brie; many vegetarian choices. Order made-before-your-eyes zabaglione with fresh berries for dessert; it's a knockout. The most fun you can have in a public place.

Michel's Baguette

49 Yonge Street (northeast corner of Yonge and Wellington)

TELEPHONE:
(416) 362-9991

CARDS:
All major credit cards

HOURS:
Sunday to Wednesday:
8 a.m. to 10 p.m.

Thursday to Saturday:
8 a.m. to 11 p.m.

OTHER LOCATIONS:
122 Avenue Road
(416) 944-0500

We are led by our primal senses. Can anyone pass a bakery without being overcome by the aroma of fresh bread baking? And when they're baking dark rye, light rye, caraway rye, marble rye, and pumpernickel; breads topped with onions, sesame seeds, or poppy seeds; breads that are braided, folded, or twisted; round loaves, long baguettes, flatbreads, and filled breads; focaccia, olive or rosemary Calabrese, and potato bread; croissants, danishes, and other fancy stuff — the passionate breadlover will follow his nose to fulfilment. If there is a bakery in heaven that uses all-natural products, this is the model.

All good things come in threes, and this new concept is a triple-header. A café buffet; a take-away "grab and go"; a bistro in spacious sur-roundings with lots of windows and wall murals. Do they have grilled sandwiches (panini) as well as cold sandwiches and wraps? As many as all the lights on Broadway, my friend. And for less than a toonie, you can get a side salad too.

But truth is stranger than fiction. Some people don't like sandwiches. Okay. There is pasta and pizza enough to delight any Italophile, as well as hearty Canadian entrées. The flaky pastry pot pie and braised lamb shank with garlic mashed potatos will even please your fussy Aunt Em.

P.J. O'Brien, The City Pub

39 Colborne Street (behind the King Edward Hotel)

TELEPHONE:
(416) 815-7562

CARDS:
All major credit cards

HOURS:
Monday to Thursday:
11 a.m. to midnight

Friday and Saturday:
11 a.m. to 1 a.m.

Closed Sunday

The polished wood of floors, furniture, and mouldings gleams a hospitable welcome. The collection of antique musical instruments in a display case is just one of the touches that would make a stranger think this pub had been here for an age. Not so, but the ghosts of its previous inhabitant, a steak house, are long gone, replaced by lively servers and an even more engaging kitchen.

The most exciting thing about this Irish pub is that it has come along on a wave of Celtic-mania. Where else would you dream of going before or after a stirring evening of Celtic music? A glass of Guinness or Harp is almost mandatory. Add to that a dozen and a half mussels steamed with Kilkenny ale and topped with leeks, and dessert of bread pudding steeped in whiskey and custard just like Granny made. You'll feel as Irish as if you'd kissed the Blarney Stone.

Upstairs there's a smaller bar with a menu of oysters, smoked salmon, and filet of beef that will charm you into coming back time and time again. It's the culture that gets you. Just close your eyes and think of Dublin.

FINANCIAL DISTRICT

Shopsy's Deli

33 Yonge Street (at Front)

TELEPHONE:
(416) 365-3333

CARDS:
All major credit cards

HOURS:
Monday to Wednesday:
7 a.m. to 11 p.m.

Thursday and Friday:
7 a.m. to midnight

Saturday and Sunday:
8 a.m. to 11 p.m.

OTHER LOCATIONS:
284 King Street West
(416) 599-5464

1535 Yonge Street
(north of St. Clair)
(416) 967-5252

In 1945, when Izzy, Sam, and Dave Shopsowitz came into the business that was started by their parents in 1921, you'd pay eight cents for a corned beef sandwich. Today, Shopsy's is owned by a giant conglomerate and you pay a few dollars for the same sandwich. Times have changed and so have prices, but generations of fressers have made this one of the city's most popular delis. Big briskets of aromatically spiced corned beef are freshly cooked every day. Thinly sliced, piled on rye bread, and slathered with sweet mustard, this sandwich fills an inner hunger like nothing else.

We all have favourites here. The beef and barley soup has no equal; and many are obsessive about the Shopsy's hotdog, steamed and served in a poppy-seed bun with any condiment you can dream up. At lunchtime, Bay Street's pinstripe-suit crowd devours salads and toasted bagels. At dinnertime, pre-theatre hordes go for grilled chicken or beef brisket. If theatre is not on your schedule and you'd like an evening meal, I'd recommend getting there after 8 p.m.

Shopsy's Sunday brunch is legendary. No surprise. Where else in the Financial District can you get decent salami and eggs with a side of fries and carrot cake for dessert?

Blue Begonia

1276 Yonge Street

TELEPHONE:
(416) 921-9077

CARDS:
All major credit cards

HOURS:
Monday to Friday:
Lunch:
11:30 a.m. to 2:30 p.m.

Dinner:
5 p.m. to 10 p.m.

Saturday:
5 p.m. to 10 p.m.

Sunday:
Brunch:
11 a.m. to 2 p.m.
(Winter only:
November to April)

Dinner:
5 p.m. to 10 p.m.

When the sign painter asked for the name of the restaurant so that he could make the sign, Sam Chong meant to say Blue Gardenia. Instead, he said Blue Begonia — and so it stands today. A favourite neighbourhood haunt, this totally cheery blue and yellow, two-floor bistro offers fresh-market, eclectic cuisine. What does that mean? Basically, it means that the menu is never boring. And Sam is always there to charm the customers — new or old.

A $21 fixed-price menu will get you two courses: appetizer and main course or main course and dessert. The smart couple will know how to deal with that to their best advantage. "You can share my appetizer if you let me share your dessert," is a good way to really get to know your dining partner. So what are the choices? The favourite is the Blue Begonia salad with greens, grilled veggies, sun-dried tomatoes, artichokes, herbed croutons, sultanas, and chèvre slicked with roasted tomato and balsamic vinaigrette. Looks like they haven't left anything out. Or there's chicken liver mousse on toasted baguette, or zesty teriyaki grilled calamari on a bed of greens. Main courses are satisfying: crunchy chicken, rainbow trout, or inventive fusilli, tortellini, and agnolotti. As for dessert, wouldn't you expect a surprise from a Blue Begonia?

Bregman's Bakery Restaurant

1560 Yonge Street (in Delisle Court)

TELEPHONE:
(416) 967-2750

CARDS:
All major credit cards

HOURS:
Sunday to Thursday:
7 a.m. to 11 p.m.

Friday and Saturday:
7 a.m. to midnight

There's no gloom that can't be cured by a hot dinner and a cool movie. Or a hot movie and a cool dinner. Across the street from Bregman's, a movie house flashes its marquee. We've got an hour to eat before showtime. Passing through the bakery to get to the restaurant is a tough trip. The air is perfumed with the aroma of cookies baking. It's a few stairs up to the restaurant.

We start with raw veggies and dip: giant white mushrooms, carrots, green pepper, tomato, broccoli, and cauliflower — more than you'd get at the market for the price. Our perky waitress is menu-fluent. Looking for low calorie? Chicken stir-fry made with pineapple juice instead of oil. Prefer vegetarian? Meatless chili on a pile of linguine. You pay small change for big extras on the half-pound char-broiled beef burgers with all the trimmings. Pumpernickel Chili is a knockout. They slice the top off a loaf of black bread, hollow it, fill it with chili, top with melting Swiss and cheddar cheese, and serve with a side of spinach or Caesar salad. Too much to finish but too good to leave. If you've never had a New York-style Reuben sandwich, this is a meal you won't soon forget. Lean corned beef, Swiss cheese, sauerkraut, and lots of chunky Russian dressing are piled between slices of pumpernickel and grilled. Of course, it comes with fries. Dessert? A bag of chocolate chip cookies from the bakery will do just fine. Now, we can sit through a double feature.

Café Pleiade

557 Mount Pleasant Road (south of Manor)

TELEPHONE:
(416) 486-5207

CARDS:
All major credit cards

HOURS:
Monday:
11:30 a.m. to 2:30 p.m.

Tuesday to Saturday:
11:30 a.m. to 9:45 p.m.

Closed Sunday

A long stretch of Mount Pleasant is exploding with small bistros. But not all eateries are created equal. Chef/owner Stavros Tsimicalis takes great pride in his 30-seat café, and neighbourhood regulars appreciate the undemanding, come-as-you-are ambience. Everything here is casual — except the food and service. You can choose the two-course fixed-price menu, which changes daily, or mix it up with à la carte choices. The salads are great: tomato, cucumber, peppers, olives, and feta; or spinach salad with mushrooms, orange sections, and feta. Bread is fresh and plentiful. Today, there's a whole fresh grilled porgy, served intact with head, bones, and tail. Our waiter good-humouredly gives us a lesson in how to bone a fish without destroying its visual appeal. A squeeze of lemon, and it's perfect. Pastaholics love the linguine pepperonata, with its thick sauce of grilled peppers, tomato, onion, garlic, and herbs. At the end, share a zabaglione — a warm, light-as-air whip of eggs, sugar, and Marsala wine poured into a goblet over fresh sliced strawberries. A feast for the gods, at very down-to-earth prices.

Caro Restaurant

1404 Yonge Street

TELEPHONE:
(416) 969-8571

CARDS:
All major credit cards

HOURS:
Lunch:
Monday to Friday:
noon to 2:30 p.m.

Dinner:
Monday to Thursday:
6 p.m. to 10 p.m.

Friday and Saturday:
6 p.m. to 10:30 p.m.

Closed Sunday

Caro is just what we want now. An intimate, clean, white space. Nothing to distress or boggle the mind. No arrogant servers who want to test your menu acumen. Sit at a window table and watch the traffic snarl by, cozy up in a curved banquette, or seek privacy towards the rear of the room, behind a small partition. Wherever you sit, know this: what you order will be fresh, flavourful, and of generous proportions.

Comfort foods for beleaguered souls. Every day the kitchen does a hearty soup, and salads are fresh and inspired. Goat cheese soufflé over tomato coulis, for example. The three pastas — fusilli with vegetables, angel hair with seafood, and involtini with roast chicken — are good, as are the pizzas. Ice creams and simple desserts offer sweet closure.

Delisle Restaurant & Wine Bar

1560 Yonge Street (in Delisle Court)

TELEPHONE:
(416) 960-1707

CARDS:
All major credit cards

HOURS:
Lunch:
Every day:
11:30 a.m. to 3 p.m.

Dinner:
Every day:
5 p.m. to 10 p.m.

Steve Campbell made his mark by creating a wine cellar that *The Wine Spectator* named as one of the world's best collections and by selling special wines at an affordable by-the-glass price. He even kept by-the-bottle prices realistic. His "Best Cellar List" recommends three whites and three reds — in categories of Traditional, Adventurous, and Sensational — by the 6-oz. glass or the bottle. Ask me, and I'd say they're all Sensational.

The kitchen that relied in the past on cheese fondues and raclettes has reinvented itself, while retaining the qualities that endeared it in the first place. Like the cozy banquettes and tables, and the long bar that affords a lone diner special attention. Rodney, the oyster-meister, supplies fresh mollusks on weekends; Ziggy's supermarket supplies Angus beef for an excellent steak and frites. There are lovely soups. Try sweet clams in the shell with chunks of sausage, diced tomato, onion, and leeks in a clear, brightly flavoured broth. The whole-leaf Caesar salad is made from perfect leaves of romaine topped with croutons and an assertive dressing. The cozy oak-panelled room, comfy booths, and congenial service make this neighbourhood bistro popular with the pre- and post-movie crowd, not to mention the city's wine mavens.

Fran's

21 St. Clair West

TELEPHONE:
(416) 925-6337

CARDS:
All major credit cards

HOURS:
Always open

OTHER LOCATIONS:
45 Eglinton Avenue East
(416) 481-1112

20 College Street
(416) 923-9867

This 60-year-old never sleeps, never did. It's been going round the clock since the 1940s and has certainly aged well. Experience in the kitchen accounts for a chicken club sandwich that's guaranteed not to veer from the norm. And Fran's may well be one of the last bastions in Canada for the classic, open-face, hot turkey sandwich with gravy. Fran-Burgers with slabs of peameal bacon and Canadian cheddar, and a chocolate shake — this is the kind of food that built the country.

Personally, I like the French fries and ketchup at Fran's. And never do I enjoy them more than with a plate of all-day breakfast, sunny-side up. No matter if it's 3 a.m. or 3 p.m., they just keep the coffee coming.

Fran's always billed itself as a family-style restaurant. Why does the nuclear family of the 21st century love this comfortable, homey atmosphere? The lights are on, someone's always at home, and there's usually a fresh apple pie on the counter.

Nothing in Common

8 Birch Avenue

TELEPHONE:
(416) 975-9150

CARDS:
All major credit cards

HOURS:
Monday to Wednesday:
11:30 a.m. to 11 p.m.

Thursday and Friday:
11:30 a.m. to midnight

Saturday:
10 a.m. to 1 a.m.

Sunday:
10 a.m. to 9 p.m.

From the street, this tiny restaurant sends out welcoming vibrations. You can't miss it — it's painted vavavoom red, inside and out. Seated in a booth inches from our neighbours, we find it almost impossible to escape the conversations of other diners, but in fact they can sometimes be more fascinating than our own.

The day's menu is of the "here's what I feel like cooking today" genre. The chef suggests an antipasto platter or grilled vegetables or pizza. I like the Florence pizza: besides the baby spinach (which says Florentine), they add artichoke hearts, sun-dried tomatoes, and fresh bocconcini. Red, green, and white — the colours of the Italian flag. Chicken gets sweet and tangy treatment, baked with Dijon and peaches, and the Cajun shrimp has some bite.

Seized with cholesterol denial, I choose the Chicago cheesecake. It's a big, satisfying dessert, but I prefer the kitchen-made apple crumble. When the bill comes, it's with a few slices of fresh apple, pear, and orange. Attention to small details in this small eatery makes a big impact. And the colour (red, red, red) really revs your mood.

Positano

633 Mount Pleasant Road (north of Davisville)

TELEPHONE:
(416) 932-3982

CARDS:
All major credit cards

HOURS:
Tuesday to Thursday:
5 p.m. to 10 p.m.

Friday and Saturday:
5 p.m. to 10:30 p.m.

Sunday:
11 a.m. to 9 p.m.

Closed Monday

Anyone who can decorate a restaurant with broken bits of pottery and make it look terrific must have talent. Imagine what they could do with food. It took a few tries to get a reservation but finally, early on a Sunday evening, they had a table for us. Who is filling up the 40 or so seats in this casual neighbourhood eatery? People who know a good thing when they see it. Now, tucking into a selection from the antipasti trolley, we see they're not wrong. Stuffed tomatoes, peppers, zucchini rolled around goat cheese, marinated and grilled veggies — a vast selection of traditional specialties.

"Most of these recipes I learned from my mother," says the young co-owner, who comes from the Isle of Capri. He and his wife charm the guests and alternate kitchen and front-of-the-house duties with another co-owning husband–and–wife team.

Provocative salads: homemade mozzarella melting over saucy grilled vegetables or grilled chicken, pine nuts, and spinach with raspberry vinaigrette, for example. Pastas fill dinner plates and astound with their flavour and variety: fusilli with tuna, capers, and black olives; agnolotti with a tomato and cheese sauce; penne with zucchini, onions, and goat cheese. Pizzas have thin crispy crusts and come loaded with up to six toppings or with the simple perfection of tomato, mozzarella, and fresh basil. Share a salad, a pasta, and a pizza, and you will leave in a halo of well-being.

MIDTOWN / YONGE & ST. CLAIR

Rebel House

1068 Yonge Street

TELEPHONE:
(416) 927-0704

CARDS:
All major credit cards

HOURS:
Every day:
11:30 a.m. to 1 a.m.

(Kitchen closes at
11 p.m.)

This must be the place. I think I've walked into someone's happening house party. Every stool at the heavy wooden bar is filled, there's standing room only, and some folks have brought their wee babes in arms. Why not? They're among friends.

Behind the bar in the rear, the chef is having a great time: steaming mussels in jerk spices and Hammerhead lager broth; tossing rigatoni with fresh Atlantic salmon, mixed vegetables, and spinach in vodka cream sauce; and filling the daily sandwich bread with ever-changing ingredients like smoked chicken, avocado, red onion, spicy grilled eggplant, and goat cheese. That's some sandwich.

Just past the bar, a small area of solid wood tables and chairs holds convivial groups. And in summer, they spill out onto the patio. There's a great selection of beer and it's well chilled. All this, just across the street from sedate Rosedale.

The Rosedale Diner

1164 Yonge Street (south of St. Clair)

TELEPHONE:
(416) 923-3122

CARDS:
All major credit cards

HOURS:
Monday to Friday:
11:30 a.m. to 11 p.m.

Saturday and Sunday:
11 a.m. to 11 p.m.

Occasionally, against the trend, the carnivore in me cries out for a really great char-grilled hamburger. At the Rosedale Diner, I could have my burger at the bar (too transient) or at a tiny table in the window (too exposed) or at the end of the bar in the "library" (already spoken for) or in the old-fashioned parlour (a definite maybe) or past the kitchen in the "Jungle Book garden." This is it — at a table covered with a giant strawberry print, fenced in by painted jungle caricatures, covered by branches of ancient trees twinkling with red and green lights. This is where I'll have my Rosedale Burger with lettuce, tomato, and onions, in a pita with green salad or fries on the side. Always be wary of the fine print: cheese, bacon, mushrooms, hot sauce, jalapeños, grilled onions, roasted garlic, goat cheese, and back bacon are each extra, and a Caesar salad instead of fries is even more! The coarsely ground thick and juicy all-beef burger satisfies my craving, although I would have preferred a fluffy hamburger bun instead of a pita.

Since desserts are from Dufflet, I confidently choose the Four-Fruit Pie, anticipating a divine confection. Alas, they'd been saving this piece too long past its prime. Next time I'll take a look in the dessert counter before I commit. Still, I got the hamburger I came for, didn't I, so what's my beef?

The Sports Centre Café

49 St. Clair Avenue West (at Yonge)

TELEPHONE:
(416) 928-9525

CARDS:
All major credit cards

HOURS:
Every day:
11 a.m. to 2 a.m.

(Kitchen closes at midnight)

Did you hear the story about the armchair athlete who fell asleep and had a dream? He was in an upscale café/gym/bar. Three satellite dishes transmitted worldwide sports programming on 41 TV monitors of all sizes, some in private booths, some measuring 12 x 16 feet — hey, even one above the urinals. He saw every pitch, every faceoff, and every goal simultaneously. To stretch the old bod he could shoot pool, play bubble hockey, pinball, darts, backgammon, Nintendo, or try one-on-one basketball in a fenced-in court. And there were about 300 others there, some in suits straight from the office. Even his wife liked the place.

And when they were hungry or thirsty, an enthusiastic server brought them Caesar salad, pastas, burgers, juicy steak sandwiches, racks of meaty barbecue ribs, crisp chicken ribs, onion rings and fries, clubhouse sandwiches. Sports food. Even quiche. Even cappuccino. And when he woke up, he was in The Sports Centre Café — his dream had come true ... almost. His wife thought it was a bit too noisy.

Thai Magic

1118 Yonge Street (north of Roxborough)

TELEPHONE:
(416) 968-7366

CARDS:
All major credit cards

HOURS:
Lunch:
Monday to Friday:
11 a.m. to 2:30 p.m.

Dinner:
Monday to Saturday:
5 p.m. to 11 p.m.

Closed Sunday

Garlands of pink flowers, tiny pinpoints of light, and vines cascade from bamboo trellises. A shrine bearing a carved mermaid-goddess presides over bowls of dried spices, fruits, and baskets of chilis. The scent of incense hovers faintly in the air. Sarong-clad servers carry aromatic plates of food to tables — plates that deliver explosions of flavour to taste buds languishing with ennui.

Like the rest of the Western world, we've fallen head over heels in love with lemon grass, ginger, tamarind, chilis, and lime. The appetizer platter offers an introduction to this addictive cuisine: crispy spring rolls, mango rolls in rice paper, juicy chicken satay, mussels on the half shell in curry sauce with coconut cream, and golden baskets (crunchy shells filled with spicy chicken and bamboo shoots). A trio of pungent sauces stimulates the palate. Order Hurricane Kettle, and they bring a whole pot of the searing soup to the table: fish balls seasoned with lime leaf, shrimp, mussels, crab, cuttlefish, and sprigs of coriander. Beef with basil, whole fish with fruits and vegetables, and chili chicken with cashews are all worthy of your undivided attention. Servers guide you to selections that will leave you more than satisfied, yet yearning to return for more. There hasn't been a slow day here since Kevin and Jane Lo opened their doors four years ago.

Vittorio's

1973 Yonge Street

TELEPHONE:
(416) 482-7441

CARDS:
All major credit cards

HOURS:
Every day:
6 p.m. to 11 p.m.

(Open for lunch in the summer)

When the owner/chef is the heart/soul of a restaurant, it's his personality that either brings 'em in or keeps them out in droves. Most of the people who crowd into his new quarters adore Vittorio and his cooking. Stick with pasta as a main course or you'll find your bill climbing in surprising leaps and bounds. Even though the servers try to seduce you with a gastroporn library of savoury seasonings and cooking techniques of meats and fish, stay cool. You won't be disappointed. Vittorio's pastas stuffed with ingredients of the day set a standard in this town: spinach, pumpkin, prosciutto, and mushroom. Spaghettini with clams is garlicky and redolent of fine olive oil.

Vittorio cooks with a gregarious generosity: herbs are sprinkled, extra-virgin olive oil is drizzled, lemon is spritzed. Fresh Italian flavour is what he's all about. And the man has a way with pizza — cheese or no cheese, tomato sauce or no tomato sauce — they're never boring.

The restaurant is small and becomes noisy on peak nights. After all, good food and fun go together. Tablecloths and napkins are clean and starched, candles add flickers and shadows of romance, and good Italian wines by the glass only add to the ambience.

Wylie's

1234-A Yonge Street (south of St. Clair)

TELEPHONE:
(416) 920-9063

CARDS:
All major credit cards

HOURS:
Every day:
11 a.m. to 2 a.m.

On the border between Rosedale and the rest of the world, this is one of the city's most civilized pubs. "This place," says the manager, "was specially designed *not* to look like a British pub." True. The ambience in this high-spirited American-style bar is definitely Philadelphia or Boston.

The friendly atmosphere attracts the thirty- and forty-somethings who have learned the value of a dollar. They've been out earning it. They tell me that the wings and ribs, pasta and perogies, are among the best in town. This is the place they can stop after work before heading home, just to sip a Corona with lime, a Sleeman's, or any one of the vast number of local and imported brews, and catch up on local gossip. I grab a stool by the window and try to get a handle on what goes on here. "Excuse me," I smile at the dark blue suit with striped tie standing next to me, "do you come here often?" "Yes," he replies, emphatically showing me his wedding band, "and I'm meeting my wife here for dinner."

Cuisine of India

5222 Yonge Street (north of Sheppard)

TELEPHONE:
(416) 229-0377

CARDS:
All major credit cards

HOURS:
Lunch:
Every day:
11:30 a.m. to 2:30 p.m.

Dinner:
Sunday to Thursday:
5:30 p.m. to 9:45 p.m.

Friday and Saturday:
5:30 p.m. to 10:30 p.m.

Chef Shishir Sharma's garam masala, a spice mixture as personal as a fingerprint, is part of what makes Cuisine of India truly the best Indian restaurant in Toronto. Trained in classic French, Italian, and Chinese cooking, he's now turned his skills to the traditional Punjabi dishes of his homeland. In this two-room suburban restaurant Sharma holds court in a glassed-in open kitchen. He slaps a ball of dough with his hands to flatten it, thrusts it onto a smooth, round rock, and lowers it into the depths of the tandoor. In moments, flat naan bread, puffy and crusty with a soft buttery centre, is brought to the table wrapped in cloth napkins.

Servers have more than a passing acquaintance with the menu, and are all culinary ambassadors of their country. But it's the tandoor oven that's the star of the show. We see the chef lift a whole salmon trout from its marinade, fit it onto a forged steel skewer and plunge it into the tandoor. A server rushes towards us, carrying a sizzling platter aloft. It is the fish, resting on a julienne of raw vegetables, its skin dark and crackling, perfuming the air with heady spices. A whole leg of lamb, halved chicken breasts, and giant shrimp all get this exquisite cooking treatment. Elaborate presentations with rich and diverse seasonings show off Sharma's uncanny ability to proportion spices. Indian desserts have an elusive appeal. You might want to try the refreshing pistachio and honey or mango and honey ice cream.

Duff's Famous Wings

1604 Bayview Avenue

TELEPHONE:
(416) 544-0100

CARDS:
All major credit cards

HOURS:
Monday and
Wednesday:
11 a.m. to 11 p.m.

Tuesday and Thursday:
11 a.m. to midnight

Friday and Saturday:
11 a.m. to 1 a.m.

Sunday:
noon to 11 p.m.

In the 1940s, '50s, and '60s our parents would shuffle off to Buffalo to Duff's for a big basket of medium-hot wings and a bottle of American beer. The place has been open for over 50 years and is still operated by the same family in the same location. But since we've become a global village, Duff's has come here, to us. Now, there's no reason to go to Buffalo at all, except maybe for a Bills' home game. But never mind. Here you'll read about food, not sports.

Should we have a steak sandwich, grilled chicken breast, or a BLT? No, we're here for the wings. These honey garlic wings have everything going for them — crispy, meaty, juicy, and as hot as we like them. In fact, between the four of us, they seem to fly right out of the basket.

"Don't let the owners see I've given you extra coleslaw," says our cute waiter, "I'll lose my job."

He uses that line with everyone, say the twins, owners Rob and Hy Erlich. And we thought we were seeing double! The Erlichs went from the socks business to the wings business. Only fitting, since twins, socks, and wings all come in pairs.

Mandarin

1027 Finch Avenue West (at Dufferin)

TELEPHONE:
(416) 736-6000

CARDS:
All major credit cards

HOURS:
Lunch:
Every day:
noon to 3 p.m.

Dinner:
Monday to Thursday:
5 p.m. to 9:30 p.m.

Friday:
5 p.m. to 10:30 p.m.

Saturday:
4 p.m. to 10:30 p.m.

OTHER LOCATIONS:
2200 Yonge Street
(at Eglinton)
(416) 486-2222

1255 The Queensway
(416) 252-5000

3105 Dundas Street
West, Mississauga
(905) 569-7000

200 Queen's Plate
Rexdale
(416) 746-6000

2206 Eglinton Avenue
East, Scarborough
(416) 288-1177

Other locations in
Brampton, Burlington,
Hamilton, London,
and Pickering

More smiles per square metre than you'd get at a dentists' convention. If you're not overcome by the friendliness, you'll at least be weak at the knees at the sight of this smorgasbord of Chinese food. The options are endless. First, heap your plate with salad bar selections and large shrimp in the shell. Then, attack the hot-and-sour soup or the chicken wonton soup, or both. No MSG. No preservatives. So clean, it squeaks.

Eager to please, the servers explain each dish, and insist you come back for more. Honey-garlic ribs, deep-fried shrimp and wings, breaded chicken, egg rolls, spring rolls, sweet-and-sours, chicken balls, fried rice, chicken curry, mixed vegetable and seafood stir-fries — I could go on. Would you believe there's even sliced beef in gravy and roast potatoes? Desserts include Jello, tarts, bars, and ice cream. Fortune cookies have bilingual inserts.

NORTH OF LAWRENCE

Mazzone's Antipasti Ristorante

4918 Yonge Street (south of the Ford Centre)

TELEPHONE:
(416) 250-8728

CARDS:
All major credit cards

HOURS:
Monday to Thursday:
11 a.m. to 11 p.m.

Friday and Saturday:
11 a.m. to midnight

Sunday (May to
September):
5 p.m. to 10 p.m.

The welcome here is so warm, you'll wonder if you've met these friendly people before. What the owners love even more than cooking is watching their guests enjoy the food. And there's so much to choose from. Living up to its name, the array of antipasti is positively thrilling. In fact, I could make a meal out of samplings of grilled and marinated veggies, salads, olives, seafood, and good fresh bread. Come summer, stop here for picnic take-out.

Some people like the front room, but I prefer the coziness in the inner room, away from the opening and closing door. Prepare to be overwhelmed by the family-size portions of pasta. Rigatoni, spaghettini, and fettuccine all come with homemade sauces, but plain olive oil, garlic, and herbs are sometimes sauce enough.

We're charmed by the polished wood floors, rustic brick walls, and bright Italian chotchkes. Heavy wood tables and chairs are a casual invitation to relax, order a bottle of house wine, and embrace the laid-back Italian ambience.

McSorley's Saloon and Grill

1544 Bayview Avenue

TELEPHONE:
(416) 932-0655

CARDS:
All major credit cards

HOURS:
Every day:
11:30 a.m. to 2 a.m.

This is the kind of place where they give you a big bowl of peanuts in the shell and you just toss the shells on the floor as you eat them. The message is: come as you are, no eye makeup or shirt and tie required. What you do need is an appetite and a couple of pals. When one of you is hungry for a big salad and the other craves nachos and cheese, sour cream, and hot salsa, this is the place.

Now that your eyes have adjusted to the semi-light, you can make out the pinball machines, TV sets, and funky lamps. Try ordering The Big Combo and settle in for a big feed. Hot garlic toast and a side salad keep your appetite in check while they put it all together: sticky barbecued ribs, chicken wings, roasted potato skins, spring rolls. Jalapeño peppers filled, battered, and deep-fried are my favourite, and there are plenty of good fries.

This is a friendly, noisy neighbourhood spot where you can't help but have a good time. You've been warned!

La Mexicana Restaurant

3337 Bathurst Street

TELEPHONE:
(416) 783-9452

CARDS:
All major credit cards

HOURS:
Lunch:
Monday to Friday:
11 a.m. to 3 p.m.

Dinner:
Monday to Friday:
5 p.m. to 10 p.m.

Saturday and Sunday:
4 p.m. to 10 p.m.

Bienvenido. I give in to a craving for guacamole, that wondrous blend of avocado, onion, and garlic. So I head for the Hassidic section of Bathurst Street — does that surprise you? — to La Mexicana's bright green awning.

The first basket of nachos and homemade salsa is a gift. On a summer's eve, we can chill out with a California chili pepper stuffed with cheese, batter-fried, and set in a bowl of tomato salsa. Or Sopa de Lima, a zesty tomato broth with chunks of chicken, melting jack cheese, lime, and a tortilla. A whole meal is Berenjena a la Mexicana — eggplant slices baked in layers of wheat germ, tomato sauce, cheese, and sour cream. House specials like these come with rice, refried beans in a crispy taco basket, and salad. With fresh, crunchy veggies, a fiesta of flavours, and a chilled litre of fruity sangria, who cares if the rhythm of the service is "Mañana."

Café Nicole

45 The Esplanade (at Church)

TELEPHONE:
(416) 367-8900

CARDS:
All major credit cards

HOURS:
Every day:
6 a.m. to midnight

Rush, rush. No time to eat dinner when you're almost late for the theatre. That's how we ended up here with a delicious bowl of cheese-baked onion soup and a glass of white wine pre-theatre, and the remainder of our dinner post-theatre. This delightful café is on the main floor of Novotel, and its lacy curtains and wood furniture give it the pleasant look of rural France.

The fixed-price theatre menu offers soup du jour or salad; steak and frites, mussels and frites, or pasta of the day; and a good cappuccino. Chicken club sandwich on country bread comes sliced in thirds, satisfying and yummy, with frites. The deliciously greasy Croque Monsieur — grilled ham and cheese — is partnered with a tangle of frites as well. There's a different bistro special every day, ranging from cassoulet to bouillabaisse to blanquette de veau. Frankly, the kitchen is not inspired, but they do serve a decent meal. And when your evening's main event is the theatre, you'll make a wise choice in dining here.

OLD TOWN OF YORK / ST. LAWRENCE

C'est What?

67 Front Street East (at Church)

TELEPHONE:
(416) 867-9499

CARDS:
All major credit cards

HOURS:
Monday to Thursday:
noon to 2 a.m.

Friday:
noon to 3 a.m.

Saturday:
11:30 a.m. to 3 a.m.

Sunday:
2 p.m. to 1 a.m.

At this below-the-stairs funhouse, anything goes and everything does. The yin-yang logo gives you a clue. At lunch, young professionals nibble on exotic salads and wonderful goodies stuffed into pitas, but when the sun goes down, things change. Jazz, blues, folk, and rock is performed by local musicians, so if you like genre-hopping, this is for you. Pre- and post-theatre crowds seek snacks like platters of mixed cheeses, fruit and veggies with bread and butter, tortillas, and pub fare.

Rumour has it that the kitchen is upscaling to meet changing demands. But it's best known as a casual, noisy place where they pack them in until someone cries "uncle" — and that's usually in the wee hours. There are stacks of board games for the intellectual, darts for the jock, big overstuffed sofas for the weary, good solid food for the hungry, and the pub's own beers and wines for the connoisseur. The chef shoots scattershot all over the culinary map, and he doesn't miss — except maybe with the dessert called Safe Sex.

The Esplanade BierMarkt

58 The Esplanade

TELEPHONE:
(416) 862-7575

CARDS:
All major credit cards

HOURS:
Every day:
11 a.m. to 2 a.m.

Big as a brewery, but twice the fun. Even though about 300 people can satisfy their thirst in this vast space, architectural manoeuvres provide islands of coziness. The elements are functional and handsome: tile, wood, brick, a scattering of marble-topped tables, and a huge painting that would be out of place anywhere else but here. See it for yourself.

Some will come to taste the brew. There are over 100 bottled beers and a few dozen more on tap, even, on occasion, authentic draft Lowenbrau. What goes with beer? Everything on this menu. Wild boar sausages, for example, or wild mushroom stew baked in a pastry crust. Pork hock on mashed potatoes and Flemish beef stew are not dishes you'll see on many local menus.

But in this Belgian theme bistro, moules (mussels) are king. Moules frites is traditional, and here there are at least ten different variations, all with a generous order of yummy fries in a metal dish with three little bowls attached for mayo, mustard mayo, and ketchup. Obviously, they're pro-choice here.

Megumi

9 Church Street (south of Front Street)

TELEPHONE:
(416) 365-0393

CARDS:
All major credit cards

HOURS:
Lunch:
Tuesday to Friday:
11:30 a.m. to 2:30 p.m.

Dinner:
Tuesday to Sunday:
5:30 p.m. to 10 p.m.

Closed Monday

During the controlled chaos of the busy dinner hour, the sushi chef, wearing the traditional blue-and-white headband of a master, never loses his cool. With fingers flying, he makes up platters of Yokozuna, superior sushi sets with ten pieces of nigiri and six pieces of tuna roll. That's dinner.

The tatami rooms have neat rows of shoes in front of them. In a semi-private curtained dining room, a family has wheeled in the baby carriage. But I like a table in the main dining room — the better to see what others are eating. Seems the best bet is a "set meal" that includes miso soup or salad, a breaded crispy chicken cutlet and rice, or any number of chef's suggestions. Still, I order my favourite. Nabeyaki udon is a huge handmade pottery bowl filled to the brim and beyond with slurpy udon noodles, whole shrimp, crispy tempura chicken, mushrooms, an assortment of vegetables, and a whole egg that has poached in the steaming broth.

On the way out, I notice a door that says "Private Club," and I take that as an invitation to enter. It's a karaoke bar in full swing with comfortable leather sofas. Next time. Meanwhile, I'll brush up on the words to "My Way."

Siegfried's Dining Room
George Brown
Hospitality Centre

300 Adelaide Street East

TELEPHONE:
(416) 415-2260

CARDS:
All major credit cards

HOURS:
Lunch:
Monday to Friday:
Two sittings:
11:30 a.m. and noon
(reserve one week in
advance)

Dinner:
Monday to Thursday:
Two sittings:
6:30 p.m. and 7 p.m.
(reserve three weeks
in advance)

Closed Saturday
and Sunday

I tell all my secrets. So, here's a find that's not listed anywhere — people in the know keep it to themselves. Reserve a table in the pretty dining room of this teaching facility for lunch or dinner and be pampered beyond belief. The front-of-the-house staff, chefs, and cooks may not be quite ready for prime time, but their eagle-eyed instructors are professionals.

Choose the length and breadth of your meal from the daily five-course menu. Wines by the glass or bottle. One day, it's glass noodle salad with shrimp and mushrooms, white celery soup with a garnish of chives and lettuce, spinach and red pepper salad, classic coq au vin or deftly grilled marlin with red currant sauce, and apple and custard pie. A recent splendiferous dinner surprised me: ragout of mushrooms in a hazelnut croustade, cream of celery soup, bocconcini and tomato salad, and striploin of beef with green peppercorn sauce or filet of salmon, fetchingly wrapped in phyllo crust, with Béarnaise sauce. I barely had room for chocolate mousse cake.

Don't forget to stop at the retail food store (open 11 a.m. to 1:30 p.m. or until they are sold out) for entrées, meats, and desserts — practice dishes by darn good cooks at totally unrealistic prices.

OLD TOWN OF YORK / ST. LAWRENCE

Young Thailand

81 Church Street (at Adelaide)

TELEPHONE
(416) 368-1368

CARDS:
All major credit cards

HOURS:
Monday to Saturday:
noon to 10:30 p.m.

Sunday:
5 p.m. to 10:30 p.m.

OTHER LOCATIONS:
110 Queen Street East
(416) 981-1399

165 John Street
(416) 593-9291

2038 Yonge Street
(416) 932-2221

A fresh wind blowing across the Pacific has stirred up a tidal wave of Thai restaurants, and one of the most popular is Young Thailand. The maître d' in white jacket and gold braid, like a bellman in a fancy hotel, looks dazed by the crush and rations his welcome. Considering the frenzy in this large, noisy dining room, where everyone seems filled with a spirit of excitement and culinary adventure, we can't imagine there's discipline in the kitchen. And yet, the array of appetizers has a craftsman's meticulous detail. Cold fresh spring rolls have plump fillings of chicken, eggs, carrot, and coriander. Jumbo shrimp, tails reaching skyward, are wrapped in light pastry, deep-fried, and served with chunks of fresh pineapple on a nest of crispy rice noodles. Even ubiquitous chicken wings, with fresh orange slices as garnish, exude the scent of lime and ginger.

Everything comes with tiny pots of brilliant sauces: spicy, hot, tamarind, peanut, sweet and sour. These supercharges of flavour could lift even the most mundane dishes out of the ordinary, so you can imagine what they do to these sophisticated plates. Ideally, come with a group and share so that everyone can enjoy a harmonious blend of the vast range of flavours Thai cuisine has to offer.

Azul

181 Bathurst (at Queen)

TELEPHONE:
(416) 703-9360

CARDS:
Visa, MC

HOURS:
Monday to Thursday:
11:30 a.m. to 10 p.m.

Friday:
11:30 a.m. to 11 p.m.

Saturday:
11 a.m. to 11 p.m.

Sunday:
11 a.m. to 5 p.m.

Creative, ambitious, amazingly good food in a location many might feel is not the "right" kind of place for them, concerned that they won't "fit in." You couldn't be farther from the truth. Okay, the neighbourhood is not exactly upscale, but are you planning to move in or are you interested in a meal prepared by a quality-obsessed chef who uses organics more than most and has an artist's palate? He has hand-decorated the place, and it maintains a clean, fresh aura.

Just stick your toe in the water (so to speak) and come in for lunch with a vegetarian friend. For you: sesame chicken sandwich; for the vegan, tofu sandwich with lemon-grass spread, sweet potato, and coriander pesto. Come back for dinner. Have a kick-ass cocktail of lemon zest and anise-infused vodka shaken over ice with fresh apple ginger juice. Is that good? You can start with salmon filet with vanilla tapenade over miso-dressed greens and have as a main course free-range breast of chicken with smoked tea, miso, and rosemary jus. The vegan will be over the moon with a Dragon Bowl or Vegan Stew. Trust me. You'll return for a weekend brunch. Did I mention that for $50 two of you can dine here more than once?

Cities

859 Queen Street West (at Niagara)

TELEPHONE:
(416) 504-3762

CARDS:
All major credit cards

HOURS:
Every day:
5:30 p.m. to 10 p.m.

A minor miracle is happening on Queen West. Two "wild and crazy guys" decided to do it all! Brian Heasman runs this friendly and unpretentious 28-seat café. The walls are muted green and lined with vibrant paintings. While some kitchens just play, this one, with chef Craig Lockhart, creates symphonies. They buy wonderful breads from Future Bakery. Appetizers include a dinner plate of red leaf lettuce salad with sherry vinaigrette, a fabulous Caesar, fresh sautéed mangos with melted goat cheese, and sautéed sweetbreads with tomato-caper sauce. Main courses — such as the jump-fried salmon with mango and coconut cream, served with corn-on-the-cob, crisp snow peas, and sautéed vegetables — are reasonably priced. Vegetarian pasta is a picture of health. Free-range chicken breast has a spicy peanut sauce; big chunks of grilled lamb, bacon, and veggies on skewers come with green peppercorn sauce. How can they serve such upmarket dishes at such downmarket prices?

La Hacienda

640 Queen Street West (west of Bathurst)

TELEPHONE:
(416) 703-3377

CARDS:
Visa, MC

HOURS:
Monday to Friday:
noon to 2 a.m.

Saturday and Sunday:
11 a.m. to 2 a.m.

And the beat goes on. This clone of the sixties Yorkville café is as comfy as an old sweater — a black one, of course. It's "back to the future" long hair, miniskirts, piercings, and tattoos, daily papers for reading, and mostly vegetarian offerings from the kitchen. Staff are members of the local bands that proliferate hereabouts. Claim a table near a window, and admire the works of local artists on the walls or watch Queen Street parade by.

The street-wise connoisseur who led me here ranks the chunky vegetarian chili the best in the area. And the hearty split-pea soup with hunks of pumpernickel make a meal. Big New-Mex quesadillas, tostadas, and enchiladas pack a hot-peppery punch and burst with veggies, cheese, and a choice of black beans, beef, or chicken.

Left Bank

567 Queen Street West (east of Bathurst)

TELEPHONE:
(416) 504-1626

CARDS:
All major credit cards

HOURS:
Bar:
Tuesday to Saturday:
6 p.m. to 2 a.m.

Restaurant:
Tuesday to Thursday:
6 p.m. to 10 p.m.

Friday and Saturday:
6 p.m. to 10:30 p.m.

Closed Sunday
and Monday

The eating, drinking, snooker-playing, crème de la crème, upwardly mobile, "been-there, done-that, seen-it-all" crowd has found a spiritual haven in Left Bank. If the designer had a vision of creating the anteroom to Hell, he has succeeded. Walls and floors are painted to look like they've been ravaged by floods, and unstretched canvases depict quasi-Renaissance figures: a Rastafarian shepherd with a flute-playing maiden, a bare-bosomed angel sporting a nipple ring. What to expect from the kitchen is anybody's guess.

Yet, we are surprised with a bright profusion of grill-roasted vegetables, warm and savoury, capped with melting goat cheese; a pert salad of baby greens glistening with zesty passionfruit vinaigrette; a satisfying spaghettini with hot sausage, sun-dried tomatoes, and sweet peppers. Crisp-skinned grilled chicken perches on well-seasoned corn and lima bean succotash. Downstairs, in an abyss-like room with a long bar that's jammed with dancing bodies on weekends, a few pals are playing an intense game of snooker. Morticia and the entire Addams family would find this drafty, cavernous suite of rooms quite homey, I'm sure.

Noce

875 Queen Street West

TELEPHONE:
(416) 504-3463

CARDS:
All major credit cards

HOURS:
Lunch:
Monday to Friday:
noon to 2:30 p.m.

Dinner:
Monday to Saturday:
6 p.m. to 11 p.m.

Closed Sunday

A *noce* (walnut) is like a menu — full of surprises. Open it, check the contents, and hope for the best. You won't know until you taste. The front section of this "corner-store" charmer holds about a half-dozen tables, and the dining room extends farther back. I like the sense of spaciousness created by windows to the street on two sides. In summer, there's a street-side patio.

If salad and pasta is your aim, you've come to the right place. The dishes in this casual neighbourhood eatery are honest and sincere; the service is friendly and enthusiastic; and the owners have been in the business long enough to know you can't cut corners on fine ingredients. Their expertise is on the plates: sweetly grilled radicchio, yellow peppers, and prosciutto capped with portobello mushrooms and splashed with Gorgonzola and walnut dressing; brilliant green arugula glistening with anchovy dressing and shaved Parmigiano cheese. After this, fresh fettuccine tossed with stem capers and grilled swordfish, or agnolotti filled with porcini and prosciutto and a heart-warming wild mushroom sauce. Unless you're allergic to walnuts, Noce is a win/win situation.

Peter Pan

373 Queen Street West (at Peter)

TELEPHONE:
(416) 593-0917

CARDS:
All major credit cards

HOURS:
Monday to Wednesday:
noon to midnight

Thursday to Saturday:
noon to 1 a.m.

Sunday:
noon to 11 p.m.

Peter Pan has stood staunchly on the same corner for years, refusing to become a grown-up. A haven for local artists, it still attracts the aging hippie crowd, disaffected youth from the suburbs, and smartly suited execs. Said one woman, who chose an airy table near the window rather than a prim straight-backed Victorian booth, "We're uptight enough already." Seasonal blossoms — today, red roses and purple lilacs — grace the bar, and servers wear Queen Street black. The menu is as eclectic as the clientele.

Start with cold Thai rolls — thin rice pancakes rolled around vermicelli and splashed with a tangy chili-pepper dressing — or tomato-cilantro salad, guacamole, and bean dip with corn tortillas that's big enough to share. There are five pasta selections, such as rigatoni with grilled veggies and fresh herbs tossed with garlic and olive oil, or spinach fettuccine with chicken and sun-dried tomatoes in a cream sauce, as well as a special pasta of the evening. Entrées like breast of chicken, roast lamb, or fish come with stir-fried veggies and rice, and smack of home cooking. Desserts from Pauline's Bakery are luscious: Death by Chocolate (a layered mousse cake), Grand Marnier cake, or Banana Supreme.

Picante Tapas Bar and Lounge

326 Adelaide Street West (between Peter and John)

TELEPHONE:
(416) 408-2958

CARDS:
Visa, MC

HOURS:
Lunch:
Monday to Friday:
noon to 3 p.m.

Dinner:
Tuesday to Saturday:
5 p.m. to 11 p.m.

Closed Sunday

You just wandered in after work for a nibble of tapas from their wide selection and a glass of wine, and something happened. Your heels began to click on the white tile floor, your eyes began to smile at the vibrant colours of Spain: the bright blues, reds, and golds. You want to stamp your feet and clap your hands. But alas, you don't know how to salsa or merengue. (On Saturday nights at 10:30, lessons are complimentary.)

So you come back one evening for dinner, just to get the feel of the place. Ancient candelabras, dripping with a decade's worth of wax, hold candles that flicker and drip and remind you of all those late-night TV, black-and-white forties films. A pitcher of red wine and fruit sangria sparkles in front of you, and the aromatic steam from a paella for two — a large pan of golden saffron rice baked with a variety of meats — tweaks your taste buds. (Paella is made to order for vegetarians and meat or fish lovers.) And what about that live music? The Latin beat gets under your skin and gives you rhythm you never knew you had. *Viva España!*

Queen Mother Café

208 Queen Street West (at McCaul)

TELEPHONE:
(416) 598-4719

CARDS:
All major credit cards

HOURS:
Monday to Friday and
Sunday:
11 a.m. to 1 a.m.

(Kitchen closes at
11 p.m.)

Saturday:
11 a.m. to 2 a.m.

(Kitchen closes at
midnight)

God save the Queen! The Queen Mother Café, that is. Still going strong after all these years, what started as a Queen Street pun has become one of the best Lao-Thai eateries around. But if you fear fiery flavours, don't turn away. Blander heroes are still going strong: quiche with tossed salad, tortellini and veggies with tomato-cream sauce, chicken-salad sandwich with fruit.

Under the benevolent gaze of Charlie Pachter's now famous artwork, "Queen on a Moose," and an aging photo of the royals from the forties, this 60-seat café, with a funky tufted leather banquette and cozy window nooks facing the street, plays host to girls in purple shoes and matching hair, fresh faces in black clothes, stressed-out students, and the middle-aged middle class. Mostly they come for the stir-fries that are combinations of shrimp, chicken, and veggies. Laotian salad is a mix of greens and herbs, boiled egg, veggies, and ground peanuts. Shrimp in curry sauce with steamed rice is a playground of flavours: coriander, basil, lime leaves, hot chilis, and coconut milk. Fantasy foods at very respectable prices. "Long live our noble Queen!"

The Rivoli

332 Queen Street West (east of Spadina)

TELEPHONE:
(416) 597-0794

CARDS:
All major credit cards

HOURS:
Every day:
Lunch:
11 a.m. to 4:30 p.m.

Dinner:
5:30 p.m to 11 p.m.

Which came first? Queen Street or the Rivoli? Well, they both just kind of evolved. Deliberately understated décor does not compete with the clientele. The walls are a backdrop for local artists; the restaurant is a stage for chicly attired Queen Street habitués, hip kids from the burbs in search of adventure, and those of a certain age with eclectic tastes. Some nights the backroom entertainment (Big Sugar, Corky and the Juice Pigs) draws local celebrities, such as Jane Siberry, Rebecca Jenkins, or The Barenaked Ladies. Now, they've added poolroom culture to the Rivoli repertoire with 13 vintage tables upstairs.

With all this, you'd think they wouldn't care much about the food. Wrong! This kitchen has been the matchmaking headquarters for a love affair between foreign spices and organic local produce, creating an energetic menu that spans the entire Pacific Rim and Western Europe. Haitian Voodoo Chicken — marinated, grilled, and sauced with pizzazz — comes complete with veggies; the pad thai is loaded with chicken, shrimp, sprouts, and other goodies; dishes such as Laotian spring rolls, Japanese egg noodles, and Chinese dumplings are a thrill for vegetarians; and if you love Italian, you'll find comfort in crostini and capellini. For the wary, there's grilled cheese and tomato sandwiches. On summer nights, the patio is a stage for the "see and be scene."

QUEEN STREET WEST

San Korean Restaurant

676 Queen Street West

TELEPHONE:
(416) 214-9429

CARDS:
All major credit cards

HOURS:
Tuesday and
Wednesday:
11:30 a.m. to 9:30 p.m.

Thursday and Friday:
11:30 a.m. to 10 p.m.

Saturday:
noon to 10 p.m.

Sunday:
5 p.m. to 9:30 p.m.

What's your favourite flavour: sweet, salty, sour, bitter, or spicy? If you've answered yes to all the above, head over to this sleek pencil-case of a restaurant. A fine bamboo curtain divides kitchen from dining room, and the pale woods, mint green walls, brick, stone, and concrete design elements are modern and natural. Not at all like the traditional Korean spots on Bloor West.

The lines are often blurred between Korean and Japanese cuisine. Miso soup has a Korean name, Dweng Chang. Try the sashimi salad. It's a delightful bowl of lettuce dressed with tart apple vinaigrette, creating a puffy bed for silken tuna and salmon sashimi. Allay your fears about deep-fried dumplings. Here, they're crisp, grease-free, and plump with a chewy mix of garlic/ginger-seasoned meat. I can't get used to Kalbi, a big slice of marinated, seasoned beef that comes connected to the cross-cut rib bones. But there's a lot of good eating here, any way you slice it.

Squirly's Bar & Grill

807 Queen Street West

TELEPHONE:
(416) 703-0574

CARDS:
All major credit cards

HOURS:
Monday to Friday:
noon to 1 a.m.

Saturday and Sunday:
11 a.m. to 1 a.m.

The search for a place to eat on Queen Street West is as difficult as finding hay in a haystack. Thai, Italian, French, diner food — any whim can be instantly satisfied. But sometimes, in the more trendy cafés, you get attitude with your appetizer. Squirly's runs on friendly vibrations. Here, they don't care what you wear, or how you wear your hair. In this tiny 24-seat eatery, generous portions of fresh food, prepared and served with ease, are the order of the day. Just so we don't take the place too seriously, there are a few whimsical touches, like leopard spots on the ceiling and a leopard-skin bar, red velour bar stools, and a mesh hammock holding some unrecognizable objects — is that a mermaid?

The kitchen seems to work best with chicken. You can get it marinated in teriyaki sauce and grilled, or stir-fried with lots of veggies and rice. Vegetarians will like Baja-style soft tortillas filled with mushrooms, two kinds of cheese, and salsa. They add a side of your choice of salad. Of the vast selection of everyone's favourite pastas, try the one with chicken and mushrooms in a brandy-garlic sauce. If the weather permits, sit out on the back patio. Feel those friendly vibes?

Sushi Bistro

204 Queen Street West (east of McCaul)

TELEPHONE:
(416) 971-5315

CARDS:
All major credit cards

HOURS:
Monday to Thursday:
Lunch:
noon to 2:45 p.m.

Dinner:
5 p.m. to 10 p.m.

Friday and Saturday:
noon to 11:30 p.m.

Closed Sunday

Sushi Bistro is a sea of calm in the erratic, pop-crazed terrain of Queen Street West. Ponder the mysteries of the balancing halogen lamps over a warm cup of sakè. Experience the seductive subtleties of eating flying-fish roe. Feast on deep-fried soft-shell crabs, tempura shiitake mushrooms stuffed with shrimp, grilled chicken teriyaki, and Korean-style grilled beef.

If you're dining alone, sit at the sushi bar and watch the chef make sushi with a slap of rice on the palm, a potent dab of wasabi, and a slice of tuna that was swimming in icy water just days ago. The menu can be dizzying, but there's a photo of each item, so what you see is what you get. Entrées like sushi or sashimi "University" (a selection of a dozen different pieces) include soup, salad, appetizer, rice, and tea. After you've mastered the art of eating miso soup with chopsticks, nothing will faze you. Well, until you try the karaoke bar upstairs.

The Swallow

1544 Queen Street West

TELEPHONE:
(416) 535-1811

CARDS:
All major credit cards

HOURS:
Sunday:
10 a.m. to 4 p.m.

Monday:
10 a.m. to 5 p.m.

Tuesday to Saturday:
10 a.m. to 10 p.m.

Born with buzz, this haven for hip and uber-cool urbanites is of and for today's youth. It will have its moments, until the youth of tomorrow decide it's very five minutes ago.

Go now, and feel part of the scene. It's called "what the wreckers left behind." Red leatherette stools line the bar; the media centre is an old wooden ice box; a white enamel stove provides storage for bottled sauces; eight tables and chairs culled from a multitude of garage sales flaunt their differences as a cohesive decorating scheme.

You'll be quite comfortable if you take rudeness for granted. Hey babe, it's the 21st century, that's the way it is. And yet, the food is tasty. Caesar salad has a dressing that bites back; earthy root vegetable soups are as silken as they are sincere; warm wild mushrooms benefit from greens and creamy miso sauce. I'm happy to make a meal of appetizers and maybe share a main course. To order a traditional three-course meal would immediately peg me as a fuddy-duddy tourist in lotus-land.

Swan Restaurant

892 Queen Street West

TELEPHONE:
(416) 532-0452

CARDS:
All major credit cards

HOURS:
Monday:
10 a.m. to 5 p.m.

Tuesday to Saturday:
10 a.m. to 10 p.m.

Sunday:
10 a.m. to 4 p.m.

This is how the West was won. Queen Street West, that is. Give an energetic group of talented young people a good space, and they'll work it. The Swan has been around since the '40s and so had its layers of, uh, "character." They scraped, waxed, painted, and varnished. They planted tulips in the window boxes, and re-opened for business.

Outsiders might find it tough to walk into a place that seems to cater to a hip crowd. You can always sit in a booth. I find that service is, well, "nice" — a word and way of being in the world that's gotten lost in the shuffle over the years. The servers here all have a neighbourly, hope-you're-enjoying-yourself attitude.

Try the homey beef ribs marinated in marmalade and beer or the trendy vegan compilations. A vintage Coca-Cola cooler packed with ice makes a spiffy bar for Adam Colquhoun's "Oyster Boy" oysters and all his zesty sauces.

Taro

492 Queen Street West (east of Bathurst)

TELEPHONE:
(416) 504-1320

CARDS:
All major credit cards

HOURS:
Lunch:
Every day:
11 a.m. to 4 p.m.

Dinner:
Sunday to Wednesday:
6 p.m. to 11 p.m.

Thursday to Saturday:
6 p.m. to midnight

(Kitchen closes from
4 p.m. to 6 p.m.)

We all hope to discover the perfect little restaurant where the food is great, the portions are generous, the lights are low, and the jazz is cool. Where servers don't rush you, patronize you, or interrupt your most fascinating stories. A place where you and a friend can sink into the privacy of a big booth and discuss the most intimate details of your lives without being overheard. Welcome to Taro.

There are earthy, full-bodied soups such as leek and potato, a warm salad of goat cheese rolled in walnuts and served on a bed of greens, a well-dressed Caesar. Of the appetizers, the linguine with spinach, goat cheese, and oyster mushrooms and the innovative prosciutto crostini are winners. Grilled vegetable pizza with Emmenthal cheese and a pile of green salad lifts this humble pie far above standard fare. The best value here is marinated chicken brochette: a whole grilled chicken breast, napped with lush lime-garlic sauce, accompanied by pesto linguine and grilled vegetables. Watch the copper mobiles sway gently near the two-story glass front. Check out the chefs preparing your food in the open kitchen. Or just sit back and congratulate yourself on having found that perfect place.

Terroni

720 Queen Street West

TELEPHONE:
(416) 504-0320

CARDS:
None; cash only

HOURS:
Every day:
9 a.m. to 11 p.m.

OTHER LOCATION:
106 Victoria Street
(416) 955-0258

What's real Canadian food, eh? I'd say it's pizza. And it comes in enough varieties to satisfy Italian-Canadians, French-Canadians, Anglo-Canadians, Afro-Canadians, and every other hyphenated ethnic group in our multicultural society. Traditionalists argue that if God had meant goat cheese and smoked duck sausage to grace a pizza, he would never have created mozzarella and pepperoni. But no one's a purist here. Stroll through the long, narrow room, pass the brick oven at the rear, and you'll come to a glass door marked Executive Office. It opens to a funky, table-filled patio that's enclosed and heated in winter and open to the stars in summer.

But I'm happy as can be sitting at the counter nibbling on Funghi Assoluti, a platter of oyster mushrooms sprinkled with Parmesan, bread crumbs, garlic, and parsley and baked in a hot oven just 'til they begin to release their juices. A bottle of Big Mama Moretti beer or a half litre of house wine can see you nicely through the meal, and the espresso, cappuccino, and caffè latte have a rich, satisfying flavour.

Watching them make those yummy sandwiches, I'm not surprised they do such a take-out business. There's a lot of satisfaction in taking home a panino thick with smoked salmon, mascarpone cheese, capers, red onion, and lemon, or a lush focaccia loaf filled with prosciutto, cheese, and marinated veggies. Better than going home with some guy you met in a bar.

Tiger Lily's Noodle House

257 Queen Street West

TELEPHONE:
(416) 977-5499

CARDS:
All major credit cards

HOURS:
Sunday to Tuesday:
11:30 a.m. to 9 p.m.

Wednesday:
11:30 a.m. to 10 p.m.

Thursday to Saturday:
11:30 a.m. to 11 p.m.

Someone's in the kitchen with Dinah, someone's in the kitchen I know. Go to the kitchen counter to place your order, then sit at tables topped with varnished collages of Chinese newspapers. Everything in the dining room (and in the kitchen) has been made from scratch by Dinah Koo. Always on the cutting edge, she introduced Asian spices to our daily lives in the late sixties.

Dinah's dishes are wedded to authenticity rather than bonded to cornstarch. The soup and noodle combinations, extending through the Asian culinary spectrum, will keep you coming back time and time again: choices of noodles and wonton combinations, meat or vegetable broth, with garnishes of barbecued pork, Shanghai chicken, and other goodies. Just when we thought this city's prima caterer was fulfilling all our expectations, she tells us she's doing dim sum on weekends: Chinese potato/taro latkes, for example, with apple tamarind relish. Tiger Lily's is for those of us who want our Chinese food steeped in tradition, not grease.

The Arkadia House

2007 Eglinton Avenue East

TELEPHONE:
(416) 752-5685

CARDS:
All major credit cards

HOURS:
Every day:
11 a.m. to 11 p.m.

I adore Greek food. All those luscious garlicky dips and warm homemade pita. I never tire of the nuances of feta cheese and kalamata olives. But I'm of the generation that says I want what I want when I want it. And here, there's no searching for a parking spot. The free-standing building, warm with the colours of the Aegean, is surrounded by its own lot. Jump out of the car, walk right in, sit down, and start enjoying.

Right away, there's a basket of warm pita and garlic toast and a dollop of taramosalata. *Kali orexi* (good appetite)! Take the plunge and order the combination plate of appetizers and a main-course house platter for two that brings grilled lamb chops, quail, chicken, a family-size slab of moussaka, and more. Or try the Greek specialties usually found only in home kitchens: Bakaliaros is pan-fried salt cod served with skordalia, whipped garlicky potatoes; Exohicko is boneless lamb wrapped in phyllo pastry and stuffed with Romano and feta cheese. The waiter will caution you: "We serve large portions."

Finish in style with a square of crackling honey and nut baklava and a cup of thick black Greek coffee. In Greece, the main meal is usually eaten in the middle of the day — no wonder they have three-hour lunches.

China Buffet King

22 Metropolitan Road

TELEPHONE:
(416) 321-6868

CARDS:
All major credit cards

HOURS:
Every day:
Lunch:
11:30 a.m. to 3 p.m.

Dinner:
5 p.m. to 10 p.m.

Imagine an all-you-can-eat buffet of foods that includes the cuisines of Asia, Europe, and America in an ivy-walled Olde English setting. This is the kind of place that lives in the dreams of teenaged boys after a day of pickup hockey (along with a few other dreams). And here's where you can please everyone at a once-in-a-lifetime family reunion. Even just the two of you can have the time of your life. If the dish exists, Buffet King has it on the steam table.

It takes about 20 minutes to walk around this vast space, check out the offerings, and loosely plan your menu. Why fill up on Russian cabbage borscht when there's a fresh sushi station? Barbecued chicken, mini pizzas, and Peking duck. Robust lamb stew and gentle asparagus with crab. Lasagna, a side of roast beef, and salt-and-pepper crunchy shrimp. Literally hundreds of Chinese stir-fries, Shanghai noodles, and more. Too much. But we love it.

Desserts a-plenty: Belgian waffles made to order, ice creams, cakes, squares, Asian jelly desserts. Ah me, my cup runneth over, and over and over.

East Side Mario's

12 Lebovic Avenue

TELEPHONE:
(416) 285-6626

CARDS:
All major credit cards

HOURS:
Monday and Tuesday:
11 a.m. to 10 p.m.

Wednesday to Friday:
11 a.m. to 11 p.m.

Saturday:
11 a.m. to midnight

Sunday:
noon to 8 p.m.

OTHER LOCATIONS:
Eaton Centre
(at Yonge & Dundas)
(416) 597-9797

5855 Rodeo Drive
Mississauga
(905) 502-6600

151 Front Street West
(416) 360-1917

10520 Yonge Street
Richmond Hill
(905) 770-4000

Other locations in
Ajax, Bowmanville,
Brampton, Burlington,
Newmarket, Oakville,
Oshawa, Pickering,
and Whitby.

Lost and hungry in Scarborough, I discover East Side Mario's. The menu is immense, and I happily read the magic words: "All pasta entrées include garden or Caesar salad or hearty vegetable soup and freshly baked garlic bread" — a welcome feature these days, when we're all financially challenged. Half a succulent spit-roasted chicken, sprinkled with rosemary, comes with whole over-roasted potatoes in a huge, cast-iron frying pan. The half rack of barbecued ribs (rib-rated 8 out of 10) and quarter-chicken combo is a steal. Veal or chicken parmigiana comes with manicotti or lasagna. I love this place, and so do my cousins, uncles, aunts, and nephews.

The thin-crust pizza and vast choice of pasta would please anyone. Service is genuine and caring: grated fresh Parmesan? More salad? Freshly ground pepper? It's an old-fashioned, good-value eatery like those in New York's Little Italy. But I like this one best because it's here. And I'll come back — if I can find it again!

Mr. Wong's Super Buffet

1221 Markham Road, Scarborough

TELEPHONE:
(416) 289-1234

CARDS:
All major credit cards

HOURS:
Monday to Saturday:
11 a.m. to 11 p.m.

Sunday:
11 a.m. to 10 p.m.

Can you handle a 200-item Chinese buffet with many dishes made to order before your eyes? Sit for a minute at a white-clothed table; order a 32-oz. pitcher of your favourite soft drink (at the price you'd pay for a glass in most other restaurants), Chinese tea, or Sapporo beer on draft; then grab a plate and begin.

Steamed whole perch with fresh coriander and whole fried crab with ginger, black bean sauce, and green onions are among the best items here. One chef slices whole barbecued pork loin and hacks Peking duck into meaty pieces. Another grills steamed buns, marinated salmon steaks, and short ribs of beef and pork. In one week, this restaurant goes through 3,000 pounds of mussels and eight whole pigs. Spareribs abound: sweet-and-sour, honey-garlic, and barbecued.

A salad bar, piled high with green mussels, fresh shrimp, and veggie fixings; a "fruitique" holds oranges, plums, apples, grapes, bananas, and more. Do you covet the sautéed seafood and lemon chicken on your neighbour's plate? Go and get some, but pick up some mussels with black bean sauce and chunks of beef with ginger sauce and sesame seeds while you're at it. Plenty of desserts, too, and a freezer filled with a dozen tubs of ice cream. It's so easy to eat too much, but then, you have only yourself to blame.

Alice Fazooli's Italian Crabshack Saloon

294 Adelaide Street West (west of John)

TELEPHONE:
(416) 979-1910

CARDS:
All major credit cards

HOURS:
Every day:
11:30 a.m. to 2 a.m.

(Kitchen closes at midnight)

OTHER LOCATIONS:
209 Rathburn Road
West, Mississauga
(905) 281-1721

20 Colossus Drive
(Weston Road &
Highway 7)
(905) 850-3565

At this swirling crossroads of North American culture, they've thrown together a mix that's sure to please a populace hungry for low-priced, high-spirited, good eating fun. Here's their six-point program: 1. Lots of baseball paraphernalia, including a replica of Babe Ruth's ball to rub for luck (we're near the SkyDome). 2. A funky bayou crabshack theme for people who like to eat critters with their hands, throw the remains in a pail at the table, then go wash up at the big communal sink on the wall. 3. For those not yet into stuffed blue crab, grilled catfish, or deep-fried alligator, a selection of pizza, pasta, and grills big enough to satisfy anyone. 4. A big red pool table. 5. A four-page list of wines with mark-down prices. 6. Something for nothing: a freshly baked loaf of soft white bread with hot garlic butter poured over top.

Before you cab it right over to this 400-seat converted warehouse, be forewarned. With most dishes hovering between the cheap and moderate ranges, this is the place everyone wants to be, and you could end up part of the throng lined up outside. Which is also not bad — you meet some awfully nice people that way.

Armadillo Texas Grill

146 Front Street West (west of University)

TELEPHONE:
(416) 977-8840

CARDS:
All major credit cards

HOURS:
Monday to Thursday:
11 a.m. to 1 a.m.

Friday and Saturday:
11 a.m. to 2 a.m.

Sunday:
noon to 1 a.m.

(Kitchen closes at
10 p.m.)

OTHER LOCATIONS:
Burlington, London,
and Oakville

Just when we needed a boost, we got a burst of Texas sunshine and country music. The good folks who brought us Alice Fazooli's and the Loose Moose have opened Armadillo in the concrete and glass corridor between Union Station and the SkyDome. A cavernous room, chock-a-block with Texas chotchkes, cases of Corona piled high, 20-lb. bags of Texas peanuts. They bring the wine to the table, pour it into water glasses, and leave the jug, "on the Texas honour system." You pay for what you drink. The first bowl of tortilla chips and fresh salsa is free. Feel-good Western hospitality, "achy breaky music," and an ever-smiling blue-jeaned staff — the mood is contagious. Within minutes, workaday doom and gloom disappears. The bar is packed. Briefcases mingle with gym bags under tables.

People talk to each other here. Want to be alone? Take a spacious wooden booth along the wall. Want to see and be seen? Pick a red-and-white-check-clothed table in the main room. The grub is good. Smoked wings, steak and chili soup, smoked chicken quesadillas. Chicken-fried steak is a sirloin dipped in batter, deep-fried, smothered with creamy gravy and smoked bacon, and served with fries and coleslaw. Texas fry-pan pasta, such as penne with gulf shrimp in Cajun spices, garlic, beer, and peppers in a cream sauce, actually does come in a frying pan. Is this how the West was won?

Asakusa
389 King Street West

TELEPHONE:
(416) 598-9030

CARDS:
All major credit cards

HOURS:
Every day:
Lunch:
noon to 3 p.m.

Dinner:
5 p.m. to 11 p.m.

If you're still searching for that special little Japanese restaurant where the owner will come rushing through the curtains at the back and greet you with bows and smiles, go to Asakusa. First, the credibility card: Shigeyuki Sano was a chef for the Prince hotel chain in Japan and elsewhere for 30 years. Now, he's retired, and taking a busman's holiday with his wife, Taeko, in this homey spot.

I love the chawan-mushi here: light, smoky-tasting steamed custard filled with surprises like nubbins of chicken, scallop, and shrimp and topped with intensely citric yuzu rind. The sashimi appetizers are pert and pretty as fresh sea spray, and sometimes, there's a huge hokkegai clam. In winter, it's a good time to eat shabu-shabu, a large pot of broth brought to the table on a table-top burner, with a vast platter of vegetables and meats to swish and swirl in the soup, then dip into citric/soy ponzu sauce or sesame sauce, and eat and eat and eat. Be warned: an order for two is way enough for four.

The best value, however, is the set dinner. Sano-san's special dinners satisfy eye-appeal, taste buds, and wallet.

Il Fornello

214 King Street West (west of University)

TELEPHONE:
(416) 977-2855

CARDS:
All major credit cards

HOURS:
Sunday to Thursday:
11:30 a.m. to 10 p.m.

Friday and Saturday:
11:30 a.m. to 11 p.m.

OTHER LOCATIONS:
576 Danforth Avenue
(west of Pape)
(416) 466-2931

55 Eglinton Avenue
East (east of Yonge)
(416) 486-2130

35 Elm Street
(west of Yonge)
(416) 598-1766

1968 Queen Street
East (at Woodbine)
(416) 691-8377

1560 Yonge Street
(in Delisle Court)
(416) 920-8291

Laugh as much as you want, but the big culinary news is that everyone still craves pizza. Go figure. No longer is pizza considered peasant food, not after some hotshot California chefs realized that trifles like lobster, shrimp, smoked salmon, and Brie could turn pizza into a blue-chip stock, and a wood-burning clay oven was worth its weight in gold.

Il Fornello opened to raves years ago and hasn't looked back since. Customer clamour prompted the opening of more venues in heavy traffic areas. Many go for the Italian pasta, the veal dishes, and one of the city's best Caesars.

Owner Ian Sorbie believes in equality. He's come up with pizza sano, a dairy-, meat-, and yeast-free pizza, and offers soyaccino, decaf cappuccino made with steamed soya milk — both amazingly good. But most people crave the 10-in., thin-crust pizza with big puffy blisters of dough and a choice of almost 100 toppings. Orchestrate your own with braised onions, capicolla, pancetta, provolone, hot Italian sausage, calamari, escargots, mussels, eggplant, or anchovies. Don't forget a sprinkle of herbed oil. But be frugal, for too many toppings can turn your symphony into acid rock.

SKYDOME / ENTERTAINMENT DISTRICT

Fune Japanese Restaurant and Sushi Bar

100 Simcoe Street

TELEPHONE:
(416) 599-3868

CARDS:
All major credit cards

HOURS:
Lunch:
Monday to Thursday:
11:30 a.m. to 2:30 p.m.

Dinner:
Monday to Thursday:
5 p.m. to 10:30 p.m.

Friday and Saturday:
5 p.m. to 11:30 p.m.

Sunday:
5 p.m. to 10 p.m.

"I don't eat raw fish, and you can't make me!" say the first-timers. Relax. Admire the modern grey-and-black décor, take a seat in a comfy padded booth, and peruse the menu. Broiled rib-eye steak with teriyaki sauce won't terrify a meat-and-potatoes guy, and with side orders of shiitake mushrooms sautéed in garlic butter and tempura veggies deep-fried in crispy batter, he could become a chopstick-wielding Japanese-food aficionado. For the like-minded, there are cooked-at-the-table hot pots for two — thin slices of prime beef and assorted veggies are cooked in a clear broth, then dipped in a variety of zesty sauces. A vegan will find Nirvana in ohitashi, tightly rolled blanched spinach with a tiny bowl of sesame dipping sauce, tempura veggies, and maki-zushi (rice, avocado, and crab rolled in seaweed).

The child in all of us will love the play-food aspect of the long bar surrounded by a water-filled canal upon which float miniature Japanese fishing boats. The chef at his station in the centre places savoury creations on the wooden boats as they sail along. Exotic things: fresh tekka-maki (tuna rolls), bright red flying-fish roe, pretty tidbits tied with ribbons of garlic chive, fresh oysters. You like? You eat. You don't like? No problem — another boat will be along in seconds. Ah, if only all of life were that simple.

Hard Rock Café SkyDome

1 Blue Jays Way

TELEPHONE:
(416) 341-2388

CARDS:
All major credit cards

HOURS:
Monday to Thursday:
11 a.m. to 11 p.m.

Friday and Saturday:
11 a.m. to midnight

Sunday:
11 a.m. to 11 p.m.

(Kitchen closes an
hour before closing)

The best things in life are things. At this rock'n'roll burger bar/café, every inch of the wall and ceiling is covered with glass-encased superstar memorabilia from the sixties and seventies: Paul McCartney's suit, Elvis's guitar, Mick Jagger's belt, countless gold and platinum records, original concert posters, hotel bills of the rich and raucous, autographed guitars, and enough really neat stuff to keep you starry-eyed for hours.

If there's an afternoon game at the Dome, it's simply sublime for a family lunch. The Junior Rockers and Golden Oldies menus cost small potatoes. On a concert night, it's a cosmic experience. The roadies eat around 6 p.m. Everyone gets revved up in anticipation as the D.J. pumps up the volume. They munch on the original Elvis Sandwich, direct from the kitchens of Graceland, and wash it down with thick Hippy Hippy Shakes or Joplin Juice. The Sergeant Pepper's Lonely Hearts Club Sandwich, the hickory-smoked chicken sandwich, or huge char-broiled burgers and fries are all under $10. Good karma.

Kit Kat Bar & Grill

297 King Street West (at John)

TELEPHONE:
(416) 977-4461

CARDS:
All major credit cards

HOURS:
Monday to Friday:
11:30 a.m. to midnight

Saturday and Sunday:
5 p.m. to 12:30 a.m.

Simply put, show-biz Toronto is in love with the Kit Kat. About four years ago, owner Al Carbone had dreams of making a tiny "smoke shop" on King Street into a backyard patio for coffee and sandwiches. With the encouragement of a few friends like Bill Ballard and Dusty Cohl, he put a solarium roof over the entire length of the property. Instant "courtyard café." He built a kitchen around a massive tree rather than destroy it, and created several dining areas. Window tables at the front, a long bar with stools, and a back area with picnic tables. He crammed the walls with autographed memorabilia.

On any given day you'll catch TV network honchos, film and TV stars, foreign and local journalists, producers, directors, critics, singers, and after a Maple Leaf Gardens performance, rock stars such as Keith Richards or Prince. One can't help but eavesdrop, and the info is delicious. At least on par with the food. The namesake, a sleek black-and-white feline, stalks the room like a maître d' in a tuxedo. A generous antipasto for two with seven-grain bread and a glass of wine is a good idea. Dinner of salad and pasta will give your wallet a gentle nudge — fettuccine with three cheeses or fusilli primavera, or the daily pasta special. The chef does a superb job with veal piccata — partnered with wild rice primavera and grilled peppers. Walk to the centre counter to choose dessert and casually check out who's who in the back room.

Leoni's

56 Blue Jays Way

TELEPHONE:
(416) 343-0044

CARDS:
All major credit cards

HOURS:
Monday to Friday:
11 a.m. to 11 p.m.

Saturday:
5 p.m. to midnight

Sunday:
4 p.m. to 10 p.m.

"You want Italian?" they ask. "We'll give you real Italian." This big, friendly Italian restaurant with red-and-white checked tablecloths is a place where you can dress down instead of dressing up, where the menu is small and the portions large, a place where they love kids but big enough so that OPC (other people's children) don't bother us.

Fifties music comes right out under the marquee to escort us in. Four of us grab a booth that could easily accommodate eight, and we start ordering as if we were in any normal restaurant. Big mistake. We didn't pay attention to the stack of plates on the table, nor did we take advice from our server. "You're ordering too much," he said, "we serve family-style."

What does that mean? Caesar salad for four is made with two whole heads of romaine; fried calamari is piled high on a turkey-sized platter; fettuccine alfredo would be enough for the Jolly Green Giant. We can't even finish the crusty herb-roasted chicken. The only dish that's finished is the slice of layered caramel nut cake — the yummy gooey slab cuts very nicely into four normal-size pieces. Leoni's is thinking good, thinking big.

Milano Billiards & Bistro

325 King Street West (at John)

TELEPHONE:
(416) 599-9909

CARDS:
All major credit cards

HOURS:
Monday to Thursday:
11 a.m. to midnight

Friday and Saturday:
5:30 p.m. to 2 a.m.

Sunday:
5 p.m. to 2 a.m.

This addition to the King Street West carnival of restaurants is still hot enough to curl the sidewalks in front of its open-to-the-street patio doors. Every beautiful designer chair, banquette, and bar stool holds a young and beautiful designer-clad body. The staff wear designer duds, too. A dozen TV monitors are fed by specially edited designer fashion shows. Aubergine walls (to match the 11 purple custom-made pool tables, darling) enclose tropical fish in built-in tanks.

In the lower-level lounge, the ambience is smart and sexy, and in the kitchen, the chef creates Northern Italian dishes that appeal to today's sophisticated palate. Toasted corn-bread crostini with black olive paste, anchovies, and Roma tomatoes; grilled calamari and grilled chicken; panzanella salad, best described as a tossed bruschetta. Pizzas are crisp and delicious; grilled salmon and swordfish come on focaccia bread with yummy accompaniments. Pasta choices run the gamut from smoked salmon with sweet-pea carbonara sauce on penne to linguine with grilled chicken and white wine pesto. By building this luxury playhouse, the two young owners have created a spiritual home for the "success story waiting to happen" crowd. Still, for all its glitz, prices are modest.

Montana

145 John Street

TELEPHONE:
(416) 595-5949

CARDS:
All major credit cards

HOURS:
Every day:
11 a.m. to 2 a.m.

Once there was a movie called *The Big Sky*. It was made in Montana. Montana the restaurant is big. Big room, big balcony/mezzanine, billiards, café, lounge, terrace, big TV screen, big tree trunks around the perimeter of the central area facing the big open kitchen. The menu, tables, chairs, and windows are all big too. Food is mostly delicious and portions are, well, big. The social scene here is very big. Queen Street business types, Bay Street's younger brokers, music execs, and suburbanites make up the eclectic crowd in the street-level dining room. Weekends, expect a lineup.

Food here is big on flavour, and unless you've got the appetite of a linebacker, an appetizer can do instead of a more costly main course. Chunky corn chowder smoulders with the scent of hickory and the kick of peppers, though the dark corn bread is too moist for my taste. Appetizer barbecue wings with plum dip and house salad is a full meal. Or try this cowboy dish — four hickory-barbecued lamb sausages on a hill of mixed bean salad. Chicken salad is outstanding: a whole juicy chicken breast with crispy hickory-seasoned skin, laced with dashes of pesto, on lush grilled vegetables.

Servers are attractive, charming, and sometimes get skewered by kitchen crush. Desserts are all big deals by master baker Dufflet. But there is something that's quite small in Montana — the cost.

SKYDOME / ENTERTAINMENT DISTRICT

Mövenpick Palavrion

270 Front Street West

TELEPHONE:
(416) 979-0060

CARDS:
All major credit cards

HOURS:
Every day:
7 a.m. to midnight

A sparkling ankle bracelet on the flat foot of the Canadian Broadcasting Centre — from the Mövenpick folks. This technicolour dream is a mecca for schmoozers, grazers, pastaholics, in-laws and out-laws, snobbish gourmets, the unprosperous, your darling children and their noisy kids, students of design, dabblers in clay, the rich, the famous, the wannabes, and everyone else.

They've made some changes here. Still, this place is all things to all people. The main floor has been transformed into a bistro, offering many of the dishes we've enjoyed at other Mövenpick locations. As well, there's a Marchélino, a mini-Marché, where you can eat in or take out. But it's the upstairs mezzanine where the chickens, game birds, lamb, sausages, and a variety of other meats roast on a huge French rotisserie. That's where the steaks (AAA Canadian beef) sizzle and char.

In keeping with the entertainment district, the lounge offers live music. No corner has been left unadorned in this extravagant environment, but one installation outdoes them all: the Homage to Dali (table and chairs) stands in a spot designated the Second Centre of the Universe.

SKYDOME / ENTERTAINMENT DISTRICT

178

The Red Tomato

321 King Street West (west of John)

TELEPHONE:
(416) 971-6626

CARDS:
All major credit cards

HOURS:
Monday to Thursday
and Sunday:
11:30 a.m. to 11 p.m.

Friday and Saturday:
11:30 a.m. to midnight

(Kitchen closes at
10 p.m.)

A grill-a-minute in this below-the-stairs downtown bar for uptown types. A dedicated crowd of the young and the well-dressed pack the place nightly. Sit at the bar with the pose-artists, the chicks, the scopers, and the genuinely hungry. You can wait until a table in the back frees up or start with a few small hot dishes at the bar, like coconut shrimp with Thai sauce, Indonesian satay, or fried baby calamari. Try a Tusker lager from Kenya.

Pink flamingos wing their way to a coastal paradise on one wall, while on the other, veggies are doing clever things. Once seated, order the Hot Rocks and food to play with. Thick dolomite tiles are heated in a 650°F oven and brought to the table with the raw marinated food of your choice. Honey-ginger loin of lamb, Jamaican jerk chicken, and Thai beef rolls all come with zingy sauces. Chicken-coconut lemon-grass soup is a winner, or try Pasta from Hell, if you dare.

Wayne Gretzky's

99 Blue Jays Way

TELEPHONE:
(416) 979-PUCK

CARDS:
All major credit cards

HOURS:
Monday to Wednesday:
11:30 a.m. to 1 a.m.

Thursday to Saturday:
11:30 a.m. to 2 a.m.

Sunday:
11 a.m. to 11 p.m.

Walking into Wayne Gretzky's bar after a game is like walking into the eye of a storm. Every stool at the bar holds a tush that's there for the night; tables along the wall are packed. Good sportsmanship abounds though, and anyone will let you squeeze in to pick up your order from the bar. When Wayne is in town, he's often sprawled on a stool near the entrance, schmoozing.

Sports and sports talk go hand in hand with sports food. From the Starting Lineup, which includes crisp chicken wings, calamari, and the Great One's grandma's perogies with smoked sausage, the stuff served here is a cut above other sports bars. Sitting in one of the comfortable booths in the adjoining dining room is almost like eating in a hockey shrine devoted to the life of one player. Pick your burger, whether it's chicken, vegetarian, or cheese steak, or pizza and calzone from the wood-burning ovens, and know that these have all been taste-tested by Wayne himself. But it's pasta that's still the most popular: fettuccine with exotic mushrooms in a light lemon cream sauce is called No Chokes; Ruff & Tumble is penne with smoked chorizo sausage; and my favourite, Net Minder, is a generous portion of linguine with a boat-load of seafood in a traditional clam sauce. Everything is served in either small or large portions, though the Ciao Down, vegetable lasagna with three cheeses, is one size only — huge. One of these, and you'll go out on the ice and score.

Ambassador Mongolian Hot Pot

280 West Beavercreek Road, Richmond Hill (upstairs)

TELEPHONE:
(905) 731-5570

CARDS:
All major credit cards

HOURS:
Lunch:
Monday to Friday:
11 a.m. to 3 p.m.

Saturday and Sunday:
noon to 3 p.m.

Dinner:
Monday to Friday:
5 p.m. to 11 p.m.

Saturday and Sunday:
5 p.m. to 11 p.m.

This modern structure of glass and light shines like a beacon on Highway 7. Never mind that the menu in the formal dining room has prices to rival the national debt of a small country. Just off to the side is an oval Mongolian Hot Pot counter. This type of healthful natural cuisine holds excitement for vegetarians and carnivores alike.

Each place at the counter sports a sunken cooking element. First, we choose a soup base: satay, preserved egg, Japanese, soybean, or supreme (a clear chicken broth, flavoured with sliced ginger and scallions). Now, with soup ladled into a large, covered ceramic pot bubbling away on our personal stove, we are presented with an array of sauces — hot soy, vinegar and garlic, minced fried garlic, and satay — and mix some of each into an empty bowl, creating a dipping sauce. A conveyor belt starts a circular glide in front of us, showing off its cargo: platters of thinly sliced raw chicken, lamb, and beef; seafood choices of sea cucumbers, salmon, grouper, scallops, shrimp, geoduck clam, and sliced eel; starchy wontons, dumplings, and bow-tied bundles of rice noodle; bean curd, dewy fresh enoki mushrooms, and spinach leaves. Each item is individually priced. Choose, swish for seconds in the hot broth, dip into the sauce, and devour. At the end, we drink bowls of the ambrosial broth that hints at all that has passed through it. There is something symbolic here.

Big Mouth Kee

280 West Beavercreek Road, Richmond Hill

TELEPHONE:
(905) 881-8821

CARDS:
Visa, MC

HOURS:
Monday to Thursday:
11 a.m. to 3 a.m.

Friday and Saturday:
10 a.m. to 3 a.m.

Closed Sunday

Big Mouth Kee looks like it might have been shipped intact from a Hong Kong waterside dock, diners and all. The floors and walls are industrial concrete. A wall mural of a busy river community ends in reality at a small open hut, where two tables are filled with feasting families.

"Never mind the menu," says Sylvia, an affable waitress. She shows us the main kitchen, set behind glass so we can see every sizzling plate, stir-fry, and steamed dish as it cooks. In an adjoining kitchen, also behind glass, Peking ducks hang in various stages of pale gold to brown lacquer finishes. You'll do well to order a half duck. If honey-garlic deep-fried oysters are on the menu, snap them up. There is no order of service as we know it in the West. Soup, duck, oysters, and a hodgepodge of plates create a private buffet of succulent dishes. Sylvia walks us by pristine aquariums swimming with lobster, Vancouver crab, grouper, and snapper awaiting their delicious fate, and past trays of extra-large oysters and live clams. Don't get too close to those clams — they spit furious streams of water into the air. (Oh, but they're beautiful when they're angry!)

Centre Street Deli

1136 Centre Street (west of Bathurst)

TELEPHONE:
(905) 731-8037

CARDS:
Visa, MC, Diners

HOURS:
Every day:
7 a.m. to 8 p.m.

Expatriate Montrealers have been yawning with boredom over what they call this city's lacklustre corned beef. Now that Toronto has the Centre Street Deli, run by the founders of the Snowdon Deli in Montreal, their days of doing without are over. The 45-minute drive to Thornhill from city centre is a breeze when the payoff is three inches of hot smoked meat piled on double rye, with sides of zesty coleslaw and crispy "patates-frites." The meats are all cut by hand in nice thick slices — lean, and trimmed of all fat, or medium, with just enough fat to give juicy flavour. Order an "old-fashioned" and you get the real thing, with whole spices left on.

It's been said of delis, "By their appetizers ye shall know them." Here, to know them is to love them. Pickled salmon steak is poached in a savoury brine and served with raw sweet onion and tomato; whitefish and carp are sweetly smoked; schmaltz herring and matjes herring are good too. With fresh rye bread, tomato, olives, and lettuce, what more could you ask? Except maybe a bowl of really good chicken soup with lokshen (broad egg noodles) and firm matzoh balls. There is a whole menu of traditional deli favourites, but before you feel as stuffed as a blintz, leave a little room for dessert. Crisp Moon Cookies, made with poppy seeds, are perfect with coffee, and the apple raspberry slice is a French/Jewish cousin of apple pie.

Korean BBQ Walker Hill Restaurant

280 West Beavercreek Road, Unit 3536, Richmond Hill

TELEPHONE:
(905) 709-3800

CARDS:
Visa, Amex

HOURS:
Every day:
5 p.m. to 11 p.m.

Considering your Asian culinary options, the choices are many, the satisfactions varied. Grill-and-eat-at-your-own-pace Korean barbecue is entertaining and unique. This Richmond Hill restaurant's décor implies a vast space, with a three-dimensional mural of mountain crags on one wall. On a cliff stands a meticulously fashioned golden temple, and, unless my eyes deceive me, there are scale models of Batman, Robin, and Spiderman about to leap into action.

Commandeer a polished granite table with a cast-iron gas grill sunk in the centre and order the Dinner for Two. Pert servers swiftly bring large glasses of tea, bowls of crisp bean sprouts dressed with sesame oil, kimchee of diced turnip and spinach, and rice. Dinner begins with a clay pot of seafood broth, accompanied by platters of raw marinated beef, chicken, shrimp, squid, and salmon. The grill is turned on, and you begin the process. A few pieces of fluffy tempura and a plate of green onion pancakes round out the meal, plus fresh fruit for dessert. Actually, it's a great way to get to know someone a whole lot better. People who can cook together could be friends for life.

Sababa

390 Steeles Avenue West (west of Yonge), Thornhill

TELEPHONE:
(905) 764-8786

CARDS:
All major credit cards

HOURS:
Sunday to Thursday:
11 a.m. to 10 p.m.

Friday and Saturday:
11 a.m. to midnight

In a spicy and exciting exercise, we stretch the borders of our taste buds to include Middle Eastern food. No culinary blurring of culture on this menu; in fact, aside from service that is more curt than courteous, we might just as easily be eating in Jerusalem or Tel Aviv. Haunting traditional music floats through this clean, vast space. A black-and-pink mirrored mural of exotic dancers, perhaps purchased in a moment of panic, punctuates the centre wall.

Baba ghanouj, eggplant and sesame purée; hummus bi tahini, chickpea and sesame purée; tabbouleh, a parsley and bulgur salad; crunchy deep-fried falafel croquettes; kibbee, cracked wheat with ground meat, onion, and pine nuts; taratour, a creamy yogurt and cucumber sauce with warm pita for dipping — every dish is well made. From where we sit, in one of the comfortable colonnaded booths, we can see what's being delivered to other tables. Now we have a problem: we want to try everything. We're fascinated by shawarma, marinated slices of veal and lamb, and the assortment of charcoal-broiled shish-kebabs of chicken, lamb, ground lamb, and veal. And there is a grouper baked in tahini sauce. We want it all. A combination plate for two gives us most of it in a tasting trip through the menu.

Crunchy honey-and-nut pastries with Turkish coffee or mint tea guarantees a glow of well-being. In fact, that mural is looking better all the time.

Tutto Bene Osteria

8133 Yonge Street (at Royal Orchard), Thornhill

TELEPHONE:
(905) 764-0199

CARDS:
All major credit cards

HOURS:
Lunch:
Monday to Friday:
noon to 3 p.m.

Dinner:
Monday to Saturday:
5 p.m. to 10:30 p.m.

Closed Sunday

These days, more than ever, we need good food to lift our spirits. At Tutto Bene ("everything good"), Roberto Lorenzoni succeeds in making my day. Grilled homemade lamb sausage with rosemary polenta and Gorgonzola cream, a big slab of banana cream pie for dessert — and the world unfolds as it should. This cheerful corner eatery, with its brightly painted tables and walls, open kitchen, and cupboards packed with jars of sparkling pickles and vegetables in oil, has been a big hit since the day is opened. How come? This is a neighbourhood of people who know what "good" is. Food plays an important part in their daily lives — and when they eat out, they're finicky.

And so they appreciate the crisp and tangy Caesar, the lush meaty flavours of porcini and portobello mushrooms in a toss of al dente penne, or the textural symphony of crisp pizza crust melting with the softness of fresh bocconcini and the bite of roasted garlic, the perfume of fresh basil and tomato. Most everything here is portioned to make sharing easy, even the roast veal tenderloin; just the mere mention will have the server offer to do a perfectly even split in the kitchen.

Roberto makes yummy ice creams and sorbets — the dark chocolate with white chocolate crunch is inspired, a total immersion in the cocoa bean.

Zaffron Ristorante

6200 Yonge Street (one block south of Steeles, west side)

TELEPHONE:
(905) 223-7070

CARDS:
All major credit cards

HOURS:
Tuesday to Thursday:
noon to 10 p.m.

Friday and Saturday:
noon to 11 p.m.

Sunday:
noon to 10 p.m.

Closed Monday

Look for a golden yellow building on the corner, then turn into their private parking lot at the rear. I've read the books and I'm well prepared for one of the civilized world's oldest and most fragrant cuisines: the food of Persia. The language is Farsi, and the dishes served in this friendly, family-style restaurant are simply divine. It's particularly popular for Sunday lunch.

Don't fill up on the scrumptious toasty flatbread that's eaten with chopped fresh mint, parsley, radish, onion, and feta cheese, a platter of chopped salads, and smoky eggplant purée. Save your consumption capacity for the natural charcoal barbecue of beef, lamb, and chicken kebabs. Add a generous dash of dried red sumach from a shaker on the table. Lots of "wow" appeal here. And there is a trio of unusual basmati rice dishes: saffron rice with wild berries, broad bean and dill rice (top this with a pat of butter and melt it into the rice), and plain saffron rice. Far from plain, the golden colour and steaming fragrance comes right up to kiss your nose. If you can't decide, the Sultani Kabob combination feeds two. With your coffee, indulge in walnut-sized pastries filled with rosewater honey.

But wait, there are two separate kitchens under this roof, with two full-time chefs. One is Persian, the other is Italian. We'll be back another day for the Italian experience.

Boujadi Moroccan Restaurant

220 Eglinton Avenue East (west of Mount Pleasant)

TELEPHONE:
(416) 440-0258

CARDS:
Visa, MC

HOURS:
Wednesday to Sunday:
5:30 p.m. to 11 p.m.

(Kitchen closes at
10 p.m.)

Closed Monday and
Tuesday

Charles Obadia comes from behind the fringed service bar to welcome guests. He wears the brightest shirt this side of Casablanca and a wicked-looking red fez. The family-run Boujadi café is painted in primary colours, the walls are hung with hand-woven rugs, and there's a collection of earth-toned pottery baking dishes, brass and silver trays, water pipes, and finjan coffee pots. It's all pulled together by the haunting beat of North African music.

Authentic "Cuisine Juive Marocaine" is served. No dairy products, no pork. Exciting spicing (toned down if you have your hot sauce on the side) and provocative combinations will excite the inquiring palate and pull taste buds out of the doldrums. An appetizer sampler has a phyllo pastry rolled around finely ground beef, spiced carrots, and beets; a phyllo triangle of minced beef; a delicious dense beef patty; a nicely spiced grilled Merguez sausage; and wonderful macerated olives. Try the Tagine — a quarter chicken or meatballs, peppers, coriander, onions, tomatoes, and green olives are placed in a clay dish, topped with a cone-shaped lid and steamed into a heady stew. You'll enjoy every scrumptious mouthful. Pastilla is a soft dough filled with minced chicken and baked with lots of cinnamon, almonds, dried fruit, and coriander. Honeyed pastries, almonds, and dried fruit, served with fresh mint tea or Arabian coffee from a finjan on a brass tray will put you in a mellow mood.

Five Doors North

2088 Yonge Street

TELEPHONE:
(416) 480-6234

CARDS:
Amex, Diners

HOURS:
Monday to Saturday:
5 p.m. to 11 p.m.

Closed Sunday

There's a fine line between an eccentric cook and a genius restaurateur. Gio Rana's creativity knows no bounds. And since the food is good and his restaurant does well, everyone says: Gio, you're a genius! When his first place, Gio's (at the sign of the big pink nose), began to suffer from overcrowding, he created a sister restaurant, loosely called "Five Doors North." Loosely, because it's about three doors north, and there is no sign except the past owner's "Future Furniture" and the clutter of empty cartons and tables still piled in front. But those who are hungry and in on the joke walk through to the rear and into the restaurant. They sit at tables covered with newspapers and clear plastic (the better to read the news, my dear!).

Start with a small pasta as an appetizer, or a bowl of onion soup with a goat-cheese-topped crouton. You won't be led astray by ordering the poultry mixed grill: quail, duck, chicken, whatever is on hand. And the vegetable side dishes like portobellos or rapini are done with care. Homemade chocolate cake or a Napoleon of phyllo pastry and creamy mascarpone cheese are understated and lush desserts.

The folks here have an off-the-wall sense of humour. Where else will you see a Catholic confessional as décor?

Gio's

2070 Yonge Street (north of Davisville)

TELEPHONE:
(416) 932-2306

CARDS:
None; cash only

HOURS:
Monday to Saturday:
5 p.m. to 11 p.m.

Closed Sunday

Look for a four-foot-high pink plaster nose over the doorway of Gio's. There's no sign, no liquor licence, no credit cards, no reservations, no lunch, no frills, and no décor. Clotheslines complete with pegs crisscross the room, a painting of The Last Supper features the likeness of owner Gio Rana, and black-and-white stills from *La Dolce Vita* pepper the walls. Gio's cousin Rosa Caporusso cooks, her son Vito serves and translates. They are from Bari, which is on the heel of Southern Italy, and their dialect is unique. So is their restaurant.

So why the nose? Who knows? What I can tell you is that there is an abundance of warmth and surprising single-digit prices. Antipasto Misto is a plate full of goodies: focaccia, salami, tiny fried sandwiches called fritelle, peppers, and olives. Pastas like penne arrabbiatte come with hot green peppers; the mixed seafood plate, with shark, shrimp, and crab slaw. You can finish with torta di casa or Sicilian ice cream and a pot of espresso. Gio's wife and child are around, and it's like we've been casually invited to join the family for dinner. Gio's a winner — by a nose.

Granite Brewery

245 Eglinton Avenue East (at Mount Pleasant)

TELEPHONE:
(416) 322-0723

CARDS:
All major credit cards

HOURS:
Every day:
11 a.m. to 2 a.m.

Pub-crawling around the Yonge-Eg fertile crescent, we chanced to hear three magnetic words: the Peculiar, the Bitter, and the Stout — hoppy specialties of the Granite Brewery. Home base of the Granite is an historic building in Halifax, one of that city's most popular watering holes. But Toronto is another kettle of fish, one that is less than thrilled with frozen halibut, lobster, and scallops that are ice-trucked in weekly from Nova Scotia.

In a preppy forest green and brass environment, where the crowd looks like they should all be at home studying for midterms, servers dish out bowls of thick seafood chowder, shrimp and sausage Jambalaya, Szechuan orange chicken, and broiled paprika halibut. Though the fish is frozen, the beer is fresh, natural, top-fermented, unpasteurized, and unfiltered. Go figure.

Grano

2035 Yonge Street (north of Davisville)

TELEPHONE:
(416) 440-1986

CARDS:
All major credit cards

HOURS:
Monday to Saturday:
10 a.m. to 11 p.m.

Closed Sunday

Robert and Lucia Martella have created a joyful collage of what they love most about Italy. Within faux ancient-plaster walls, there's an outdoor garden, a dining room, an espresso bar, a language school, and a party room. You'll find good talk, good food, and great bread — Italian sourdough with pesto or black olives, or soft and crusty rolls baked with rosemary. Lucia is always there, and Robert is a friend to all.

But first, you wait in line. You sigh over a food counter filled with an orgy of 30 antipasti: eggplant parmigiana, Caprese salad, artichoke and mushroom Torta Rustica, fresh fennel and baked olives, and Risotto Nero, to name a few. Three snappy choices, or seven, or as many as you wish — they are priced accordingly, and may include everything from calamari to veal carpaccio. For a main course you can choose from dishes as varied as grilled porgy with polenta and eggplant, and grilled chicken with roasted peppers and ricotta salad. And there are a dozen soul-stirring homemade desserts.

The street spills over with Italian eateries, but in the whispered competition for the palates and wallets of uptown Italophiles, Grano wins — hands down.

Grazie Ristorante

2373 Yonge Street (north of Eglinton)

TELEPHONE:
(416) 488-0822

CARDS:
All major credit cards

HOURS:
Monday to Thursday:
noon to 11 p.m.

Friday:
noon to 2 a.m.

Saturday:
5 p.m. to midnight

Sunday:
5 p.m. to 11 p.m.

No more room! Every bar stool is filled, and they're standing three deep, drinking San Pellegrino mineral water or house wine from tumblers. Still the hordes pile into this pizza, pasta, and salad bistretto, adding to the high-decibel ambience and noise level. You either love it or hate it. The later the hour, the younger the crowd. They tuck into 15 different kinds of elegant pizzas (fresh dough rolled for each order) with purely Italian flavours: Filippo with sun-dried tomatoes, goat cheese, mozzarella, Asiago, fontina, and blue cheese; Pescara with tomato, mozzarella, shrimps, clams, and basil. Twenty-five exquisite fresh pasta selections include linguine with huge shrimp and clams, grilled chicken and green onion, and something quite different, spaghetti with sautéed broccoli, anchovies, pine nuts, and raisins, covered with toasted bread crumbs and sesame seeds.

Beauties with perfect corkscrew curls and guys with a look that's lifted from the fashion pages are not just from the neighbourhood — they drive in from Mississauga and Thornhill. Why not? Grazie has what it takes to survive: exceptional food, easygoing prices, and no reservations.

Saporito Café Bakery

50 Eglinton Avenue East (east of Yonge)

TELEPHONE:
(416) 484-4846

CARDS:
All major credit cards

HOURS:
Monday to Friday:
7 a.m. to 8 p.m.

Saturday:
9 a.m. to 3 p.m.

Closed Sunday

"Amazing! Incredible!" At Saporito, these reactions are elicited initially by the display of delectable foods and secondly, by the prices, which are just one step removed from free. This cheery, brightly painted café has an eating area in front with a view of dozens of seductive fruit tarts, creamy tortes, cookies, lush cakes, muffins, and croissants, and another in the back, adjacent to the eye-boggling salads and main courses. Salads include red peppers, eggplant, chickpeas, cucumbers, pickles, broccoli, cauliflower, greens, and more. Hard choices. For me, a trio of plump marinated mushrooms, green beans, and red potatoes with red onion. For my pal, broccoli with creamy cucumber dressing. Main courses are basically Italian offerings of ravioli, agnolotti, vegetable and meat lasagnas, and all the pastas we know and love. We're intrigued by an enormous slice of focaccia, a pie overstuffed with broccoli and Italian sausage, and the veal special — two thin slices of veal scallopini with fresh tomato and green pepper salsa partnered with rice, peas, mushrooms, and a crisp Caesar with bacon bits.

Service is totally friendly, and the servers understand how people want to eat their food. We cannot ignore the siren call of the fresh fig and almond tart, or a rum and filbert brownie with chocolate glaze. Coffee in big mugs is good too. I don't always divulge exactly what I've consumed. But in this instance, the cost makes it totally relevant.

Shoeless Joe's Sports Bar

250 Eglinton Avenue West (east of Avenue Road)

TELEPHONE:
(416) 484-9934

CARDS:
All major credit cards

HOURS:
Every day:
11 a.m. to 2 a.m.

OTHER LOCATIONS:
3200 Dufferin Street
(416) 787-7781

401 King Street West
(416) 596-2171

1189 King Street West
(416) 534-3666

2826 Markham Road
(416) 291-6886

The jury of fans is still out on baseball player Shoeless Joe Jackson, who was banned for life from the game in 1919 for being one of the Chicago White Sox who "fixed" the World Series. Today, he's a sports legend, and Shoeless Joe's Sports Bar is definitely the place to eat dinner and drink up baseball with a group of like-minded folks. A jukebox holds a vast selection of everybody's favourite tunes. This baseball theme park is loaded with memorabilia, posters, a pool table, and enough hanging television sets to satisfy every sports fan's cravings. The most popular dish, at the bar or at a table, is wings. These meaty morsels come in wicker baskets with mild, medium, or suicide spicing. Another good bet is chicken fingers with ripple fries and carrot and celery sticks. Fast foods that go well with the wide world of television sports include: steak on a kaiser, bruschetta, breaded shrimp, and potato skins filled with cheddar.

The story goes that Shoeless Joe got his name because he once wore no shoes when he played in the minors. Here, there's a dress code: shoes required.

Vanipha Lanna

471 Eglinton Avenue West (west of Avenue Road)

TELEPHONE:
(416) 484-0895

CARDS:
All major credit cards

HOURS:
Monday to Thursday:
noon to 10 p.m.

Friday and Saturday:
noon to midnight

Closed Sunday

This restaurant prepares exquisite Lao-Thai dishes, matching its first location, Vanipha Fine Cuisine, the below-stairs nook in Kensington Market. Every night, this location is filled with people who don't care if they're sitting almost cheek-to-cheek with strangers. They don't care how long they have to wait for their food. They have fallen in love with lemon grass, lime, coconut, ginger, chili, and coriander. They can't get enough of the clean, bright flavours, grease-free cooking, and lovingly garnished presentations that emerge from this kitchen. Here, you'll find a dish that is one of the best you'll ever get in a Thai eatery: a half-dozen Thai dumplings of minced chicken and seafood in rice or wonton wrap, which arrive in a bamboo steamer with a tiny dish of hot sauce. Another good dish is chicken with snippets of long green beans stir-fried in a spicy Kafir lime sauce that keeps you interested right to the end. Try the sticky rice that comes in a raffia cylinder — delicious dipped in spicy peanut sauce. Pad Thai here is a stir-fry of rice noodles with ground chicken, shrimp, fresh bean sprouts, and a sweetish sauce. I love the huge silver pots used to serve steamed rice; ask for a little more, and they just smile and ladle it out.

All the orders here take time — every dish is made from scratch, and by the look of the dishes paraded in front of us, it's all worth the wait.

The Wineyard Restaurant

2110 Yonge Street

TELEPHONE:
(416) 489-4929

CARDS:
All major credit cards

HOURS:
Monday to Friday:

Lunch:
noon to 3 p.m.

Dinner:
5 p.m. to 10:30 p.m.

Saturday:
5 p.m. to 11 p.m.

Open Sundays for
private parties only

What restaurant prints "Good Appetite" on the menu in many languages: Bon Appetit, Bete Avon, Kali Orexi, Buon Appetito? The kind that's run by people who really care about their customers and bring a nice bread basket with the menu.

There is no assembly-line cooking here. Through the glassed-in open kitchen, we can see oversized platters of food being prepared. I'm mesmerized by the wood-fired oven — they could roast a whole lamb in there — and maybe they do. Pizzas come with a litany of ingredients. You can write your own ticket. Pasta can be as complicated or easygoing as you wish. And with a nod to international tastes, there are dishes that feature tandoori spicing and basmati rice.

This high-ceilinged, airy restaurant has a fascinating interior. Intricate, handcrafted railings, wrought-iron sofas, wine holders, and candelabras that are obviously one of a kind. These objects, as well as the generous cooking, show us that the people in charge here are true restaurateurs. They stay open late for us, and offer unpretentious, shareable fare.

Ba–ba–lu's Tapas Bar

136 Yorkville Avenue

TELEPHONE:
(416) 515-0587

CARDS:
Visa, Amex

HOURS:
Every day:
6 p.m. to 2 a.m.

The voluptuous beat of Latin salsa music reaches out onto the street and pulls you into Ba–ba–lu's. The bar is crowded with Margarita sippers. Fabulous sangria is sold by the glass or the pitcher. The menu has tapas: tasty little dishes (all the better to share with you, my dear) that you order singly, and that start at just a few bucks and go up in $1 increments, with half a dozen items in each price range. The chef understands food with a Latin beat. I like the grilled flank steak tortillas with garlic-potato rouille and tomato salsa; grilled chicken breast with saffron, olive, and lemon rind tapenade; the surprisingly huge serving of crisp deep-fried calamari.

And how could I not be excited about a place that's open only during the decent hours of the day: from 6 p.m. to 2 a.m. Most nights, there's a cover charge for the live music and the dance show put on by servers. Totally impossible to watch without joining in — ergo, dance classes are offered.

The Bloor Street Diner

Manulife Centre, 55 Bloor Street West (at Bay)

TELEPHONE:
(416) 928-3105

CARDS:
All major credit cards

HOURS:
Every day

Café:
7 a.m. to 11:30 p.m.

Dining Room:
11 a.m. to 10 p.m.

OTHER LOCATION:
2419 Yonge Street
(north of Eglinton)
(416) 544-1661

Sometimes, it just takes a gleaming steel rotisserie filled with row upon row of plump, free-range chickens roasting to a golden brown to make you see things in a whole new light. Maybe tonight you can ace your know-it-all friend in a game of billiards, maybe you can strike up a conversation with the group of witty-looking people sitting on the patio that overlooks Bay Street. Only one thing is certain: you can have a terrific dinner here. In the sophisticated dining room, sit at a banquette under French canvas umbrellas and start with wild boar and apricot terrine, choose your whole fish from the ice-filled display, or happily wait a few minutes while the rotisserie pork, stuffed with tapenade and roasted apples, is turned to perfection. In Le Café, the menu boasts French onion soup, Caesar salad, and Mediterranean vegetable terrine — a slice of grilled eggplant, peppers, sun-dried tomatoes, and mushrooms with garlic aioli. There's a variety of rotisserie meats: beef, lamb, sausages, and that incredible chicken, with mashed potatoes. Or eat a traditional French hotdog in a baguette or a lush Italian sandwich at L'Express, which juts out into the polished granite lobby of the Manulife Centre.

The kitchen is staffed with a crew culled from the city's finest dining establishments. This place, devoted to the here and now, offers a vast array of possibilities. Just the kind of spot that Bloor Street was dying for.

YORKVILLE

Blues on Bellair

25 Bellair Street

TELEPHONE:
(416) 944-2095

CARDS:
All major credit cards

HOURS:
Sunday:
5 p.m. to 10 p.m.

Tuesday to Thursday:
5 p.m. to midnight

Friday and Saturday:
5 p.m. to 1 a.m.

(Late-night menu after
10 p.m.)

Closed Monday

A midnight blue cocoon for grown-ups with a kitchen that sizzles and a groovy '70s rhythm and blues band, Luke and the Apostles.

Modern, below-stairs cozy, yet with an open view to the street. A big two-paged menu exudes a confidence with spices that span the Southwest and Creole/Carib. Latin from Manhattan meets laid-back New Orleans. You might consider, for a moment, pumpkin and wild rice cakes with smoked alligator tail in banana guava ketchup. But, if you're a traditionalist, you'll go for the 8-oz. Cajun beef burger capped with caramelized onions and a tangle of sweet potato fries.

The Yorkville hippie scene has grown up, cleaned up nice, and returned to its roots.

Café Nervosa

75 Yorkville Avenue

TELEPHONE:
(416) 961-4642

CARDS:
All major credit cards

HOURS:
Every day:
11 a.m. to 11 p.m.

(midnight in summer)

Contrary to its agitated name, Café Nervosa is very laid-back. "Hi, guys," smiles our server, "what can I get for you?" The cooks at the open kitchen are so casual, the cynic in me wonders if they're really cooking or just fooling around. In fact, they're preparing some of the tastiest pizza you'll find in the area. Everything from the classic Margherita topped with fresh plum tomatoes, mozzarella, and basil to a Funghi e Formaggi, aromatic Gorgonzola and goat cheese, melting with mushrooms, prosciutto, and onions.

A half-dozen antipasti include the classics with a twist: grilled corn-bread bruschetta with tomato and herbs, a handsome plate of beef carpaccio. Pasta dishes have the verve that only comes from fresh herbs and extra-virgin olive oil. I like the grilled chicken breast with sun-dried tomatoes and goat cheese.

And if you just want to drop in for a cappuccino, latte, or an Italian filter coffee and a biscotti, they're cool with that. This petite café, patio, and rooftop terrace flaunts bright yellow umbrellas that say, hey, we're a major attraction here.

The Caffè

50 Bloor Street West (Holt Renfrew, third floor)

TELEPHONE:
(416) 922-2333

CARDS:
All major credit cards,
Holt Renfrew card

HOURS:
Monday to Wednesday
and Saturday:
10 a.m. to 5 p.m.

(Kitchen open 11:30
to 4 p.m.)

Thursday and Friday:
10 a.m. to 7 p.m.

(Kitchen open 11:30
a.m. to 6:30 p.m.)

Sunday:
noon to 4 p.m.

(Kitchen open until
3:30 p.m.)

The first meal of the day is always an exercise in personal taste. Some people like to start with sweets, some prefer savouries. But there are Sunday mornings when your kitchen offers no inspiration, and no one wants to help with dishes. The pristine Caffè at Holt's is a delicious dividend on the third floor, right next to the escalator, and welcomes us with the aroma of baking, and fresh coffee. Huge, buttery croissants and custard-filled brioche; cinnamon-raisin French toast made from thickly sliced challah, served with strawberry preserves; a stack of hotcakes with thick sour cream and a ripe, sliced banana.

The designer duds enticingly displayed in chic boutiques can be distracting, but they take second place to fine open-face country omelettes with homemade fried potatoes and sausage and orange juice squeezed to order. For an extra pittance, they'll spike it with champagne. The menu is short but covers every base, and each dish is a classic. A large toasted bagel is thickly spread with cream cheese and piled with thinly sliced smoked salmon. At the other end of the diet spectrum towers a tall parfait glass layered with fresh fruit, yogurt, and homemade crunchy granola. Or you can have just a muffin and coffee. During the week the exciting all-day menu is as current as the nearby fashions. We emerge well fed, ready to give in to the irresistible temptation of the shoe department.

YORKVILLE

Cantine

138 Avenue Road

TELEPHONE:
(416) 923-4822

CARDS:
All major credit cards

HOURS:
Monday to Thursday:
11 a.m. to 10 p.m.

Friday:
11 a.m. to 11 p.m.

Saturday:
10 a.m. to 11 p.m.

Sunday:
10 a.m. to 10 p.m.

Joey Bersani greets old friends and new with open arms, finding them the right table for their mood, making sure everybody is happy (nothing fancy, lots of leather club chairs up front and a bar for schmoozing, sipping, and smoking). You can tell the quality of a place by the bar snacks they serve, and the huge bowl piled high with all my favourite Italian olives gives the right message (on an ordinary weeknight, residents of Forest Hill, the Annex, and Rosedale converge — cashmere and jeans).

You will love the delectable herb-battered crisp calamari with sweet red pepper dip; an upscale version of fish and chips with a paper cone of frites and a dollop of garlic mayo; a half Portuguese rotisserie chicken, roasted and juicy. Is there steak frites? You bet. There's even a vegan version of bistro fare in the form of a black bean and tofu pie with smoky tomato salsa.

Joey takes over in the kitchen for weekend brunch. "That's what I like to do," he says to the guests on his doorstep every Sunday morning at 10.

The Coffee Mill

99 Yorkville Avenue

TELEPHONE:
(416) 920-2108

CARDS:
All major credit cards

HOURS:
Monday to Thursday:
10 a.m. to 10 p.m.

Friday and Saturday:
10 a.m. to midnight

Sunday:
noon to 10 p.m.

Do you have a meat and potatoes palate in a pasta primavera world? Does trendy cuisine make you long for the way things used to be? Nothing has changed at The Coffee Mill since it opened over 30 years ago in the spring of 1963. Owner Marta Heczey makes sure that the Hungarian goulash, a meal in itself, is still simmered with lots of veal chunks and vegetables, and that the cabbage rolls are plump and juicy. We're still served by the same waitresses with their beautiful smiles and sensible shoes.

Saturday afternoons, stars of stage, screen, TV, and radio gather together, and literary and legal lions hold court. The Coffee Mill is an anomaly on Yorkville. While new cafés come and go, serving up the latest trendy foods at tourist prices, Marta prides herself on remaining traditional, true to her roots. First a plate of buttered rye bread. Then Weiner Schnitzel, a plate-sized cutlet in a crisp batter, served with warm potato salad and coleslaw. A crisp salad precedes Veal Paprikash, which shares the plate with homemade spaetzle. The Coffee Mill salads — greens with a scoop of tuna or egg salad — and the open-face egg and olive on toasted rye bread I've been eating here for 25 years are still the same. The coffee cake and apple strudel have gotten better, and both go well with any one of the dozen continental coffees on the menu.

Flo's

10 Bellair Street

TELEPHONE:
(416) 961-4333

CARDS:
All major credit cards

HOURS:
Monday to Thursday:
7:30 a.m. to 10 p.m.

Friday:
7:30 a.m. to midnight

Saturday:
8 a.m. to 10 p.m.

Sunday:
8 a.m. to 11 p.m.

Are you among the backlash of people who've had it with fancy food, who don't want to eat anything they can't pronounce or that Mom never put in front of them? For you, there is Flo's. Glitzy chrome, black-and-white tile, enough pink neon to give the place a glow, and, to hearken back to gentler times, there are comfy red vinyl booths, an ancient Wurlitzer, and Heinz ketchup and French's mustard on every table.

The best meal here is breakfast. If you come at other times, don't let the chicken tarragon salad scare you. It's really just scoops of minced chicken salad, crumbly white feta cheese, coleslaw, and hard-boiled egg, garnished with Cellophane packets of saltines. And don't let linguine in a spicy tomato and basil sauce worry you. You won't taste the basil in the tomato sauce, but the six medium shrimp on top are a nice touch. Of course, there are adequate burgers and grills. If you're feeling adventurous, try the focaccia, a seasoned bread stuffed with nutty cheese, eggplant, peppers, and zucchini; you'll be very happily surprised.

Indigo Music, Books & Café

Manulife Centre, 55 Bloor Street West

TELEPHONE:
(416) 925-3536

CARDS:
All major credit cards

HOURS:
Sunday to Wednesday:
9 a.m. to 11 p.m.

Thursday to Saturday:
9 a.m. to midnight

OTHER LOCATIONS:
Yonge-Eglinton Centre
2300 Yonge Street
(416) 544-0049

8705 Yonge Street
(Highway 7 & Yonge
Richmond Hill)
(905) 731-8771

Eaton's Centre
220 Yonge Street
(416) 591-3622

Yorkdale Mall
3401 Dufferin Street
(416) 781-6660

Scarborough Town
Centre
300 Borough Drive
(416) 279-1555

Empress Walk
5095 Yonge Street
(416) 221-6171

The rule is shop first and eat later. Literati and glitterati, tastemakers and trendsetters, book lovers and gift buyers — they all stroll the aisles of Indigo, selecting books and music in a place that has a friendly, casual ambience but that is also totally efficient. For pre- and post-moviegoing, the place is peerless.

Here is where the city's fashionmongers indulge their stylish tastes, leaf through the latest magazines, nibble Italian vegetarian sandwiches on the grill, and sip freshly blended fruit drinks such as Equatorade (mango, pineapple, banana). If the soup of the day is chicken noodle, order it — trust me, you'll feel better.

At the open kitchen, they hand-slice a grilled farmhouse chicken and place it on caraway rye spread with Pommery mustard; they are considerate and mix tuna salad with no-fat yogurt and cucumber, and put it between slices of whole-grain bread; they grill a luscious turkey Reuben and call out from the counter when it's ready. Add a slice of fresh lemon poundcake or chocolate squares that are as good as Mom's, and you've had the best value in the neighbourhood.

Indochine

4 Collier Street

TELEPHONE:
(416) 922-5840

CARDS:
All major credit cards

HOURS:
Lunch:
Monday to Saturday:
noon to 3 p.m.

Dinner:
Monday to Saturday:
5 p.m. to 10 p.m.

Closed Sunday

No surprise that adventurers who backpack through Vietnam return with a high regard for the food of the country. The French colonization of the country influenced the cuisine enormously, and the proximity of neighbouring China and India also left its mark. Once back at home, these world travellers flock to Indochine. It's easy to miss this restaurant, as it's tucked into a side street just east of Yonge Street, across from the Toronto Reference Library.

What does the country's cultural history mean to us? Haute cuisine at plebeian prices. Two rock oysters on the half shell sizzle in a hot sauce of butter, garlic, and shallots, and there's French bread to mop up the juices. Noodle soups, fragrant with lemon grass and tamarind, are a lunchtime favourite. And there are one-pot dishes like chicken and rice cooked in a flavour-rich sauce.

Service can be uninterested and blasé, but don't take it personally. Fixed-price, set lunches and dinners are so reasonable, I'll bet you star this page with indelible ink.

Little Tibet

81 Yorkville Avenue

TELEPHONE:
(416) 963-8221

CARDS:
All major credit cards

HOURS:
Lunch:
Tuesday to Saturday:
11 a.m. to 3 p.m.

Dinner:
Tuesday to Friday:
5 p.m. to 9:30 p.m.

Saturday and Sunday:
5 p.m. to 10:30 p.m.

Closed Monday

You've seen the movies, now you can enjoy the food of far-off Tibet. The owner of this pretty, semi-subterranean restaurant, Namgyal Gongya, tells me he considers Tibetan cuisine to be a cross between Chinese and Thai. In fact, it presents the best of both worlds. So while you're eating Tibetan cuisine for the first time, you're thinking, Hey, I've eaten this before.

Many of the diners seated at the dozen or so tables have made the trek and know that Tibet's most popular dish is Momo, little dumplings steamed or fried, filled with beef or mixed vegetables. The seasonings are subtle and elusive, but we do sense the tang of garlic, ginger, coriander, and red pepper. Vegans adore this cuisine — it was, after all, born of Buddhism. There are thinly sliced potatoes sautéed with spinach and garnished with coriander leaves; sautéed fresh mushrooms with zucchini, garlic, and ginger. Carnivores go for Tibetan lamb curry or marinated beef served with a steamed bun.

While I might chugalug a pot of Bocha, a rib-sticking drink of tea, butter, and salt, to see me over the Himalayas to Tibet, on Yorkville I'm okay with a simple coffee. And in a further effort to give us what we like, the owners have a Dufflet dessert of the day.

Lox, Stock & Bagel

55 Avenue Road (in Hazelton Lanes)

TELEPHONE:
(416) 968-8850

CARDS:
All major credit cards

HOURS:
Monday to Wednesday:
8 a.m. to 10 p.m.

Thursday to Saturday:
8 a.m. to 11 p.m.

Sunday:
9 a.m. to 9 p.m.

All the world loves a bagel — though in some Canadian quarters, they still think bagels are part of a U.S. plot to take over Canadian culture. This notwithstanding, these doughnut-shaped, chewy rolls have a lot of personality, any way you slice 'em. Newly retro-chic, this deli is expanding its horizons with designer dishes and settling into the heart of haute cuisine-ville. Breakfast, from 8 a.m., comes on a selection of breads including New York-style bagels and challah. You can lunch on seasonal salads of every probable and improbable combination — classics such as Cobb, Caesar, Niçoise, and Greek, and innovations such as spinach tossed with bean sprouts, sliced strawberries, and mushrooms. They all come with a bagel, of course. Between 4 p.m. and 6 p.m., the black-and-gold lounge is the social set's favourite haunt.

Owner Alan Cherry, food and fashion impresario, dresses his staff in seasonally correct vogue and has peppered the menu with stylish dishes. This is a deli with a culinary conscience: low-fat pizza, for example, is made with crispy egg-white crust, laden with marinara sauce and skim mozzarella, and loaded with vitamin-rich veggies and portobello mushrooms. Pastas, steaks, stir-fries, pizza, chicken, seafood, deli-style sandwich platters, desserts — they're all available all day. It's a nosher's wildest dream come true.

Mövenpick

133 Yorkville Avenue

TELEPHONE:
(416) 926-9545

CARDS:
All major credit cards

HOURS:
Sunday to Tuesday:
7 a.m. to midnight

Wednesday and
Thursday:
7 a.m. to 1 a.m.

Friday and Saturday:
7 a.m. to 2 a.m.

OTHER LOCATION:
165 York Street
(416) 366-5234

Dine out with a child, an aunt, a parent, or the whole family in this friendly, folksy atmosphere. Totally unpretentious and decorated with huge, brightly photographed menus geared to suit everyone from seniors to the highchair set. At holiday times, there are special candy treats for kids. Sit by the windows, watching the passing Yorkville parade, or on the mezzanine. There is no pressure here to order a full three-course meal. Personally, I like a few small dishes as a main course and a big dessert — ice cream, preferably. Since Mövenpick opened, I've gone through the entire menu and found a few favourites: Salade Niçoise, a plate full of veggies with a slice of pan-fried tuna; sautéed Provimi liver with onion, garlic, and herb butter, which comes with a rosti potato pancake; and a variety of grilled veal sausages. And there's enough pasta — seafood lasagna or tagliatelle with chicken, for example — to satisfy any pasta lover.

The place is still humming after midnight, and that's when I crave a tasty open-faced sandwich: creamed wild mushrooms, saucy beef tenderloin with field mushrooms, or curried breast of chicken with banana and coconut, just to name a few. Choruses of "Happy Birthday" ring out every few minutes, as they present their fabulous cakes with song to another birthday boy or girl. The only difficulty in this place is getting a table.

The Patio

220 Bloor Street West (in the Hotel Intercontinental)

TELEPHONE:
(416) 324-5885

CARDS:
All major credit cards

HOURS:
Every day
(summer only):
noon to 1 a.m.

I get letters. "Isn't there any privacy any more? Wherever I go for dinner with a special date, I see people from work, my parents, friends, or an unwelcome face from the past who insists on joining me. Am I paranoid, or is this town too small for me?" For you, my friend, there is The Patio. Enter from a discreet walkway on the west side of the Intercontinental Hotel and you'll find yourself in a large, private, quiet garden. As the sun sets behind the trees and flowering shrubs, a few lamps are lit. A tiny candle is placed on your table.

Service is prudent, unobtrusive. Passers-by don't even know this place exists. The menu is casual — as befits outdoor dining. A huge Greek or Caesar salad is a good start, or try bruschetta topped with chopped and seasoned ripe tomatoes. The California Club with fries is fabulous, as is the smoked chicken and Brie on a baguette with corn chips. Entrées include something to suit every taste: chicken and beef satays with peanut sauce, or a huge char-broiled beef burger with old white cheddar, a salad, and fries, accompanied by jars of ketchup, mustard and relish. They make interesting vegetarian pizza and angel hair pasta with grilled chili shrimp and fresh herbs. Share an outrageous dessert like chocolate crêpes with sabayon-glazed berries. No one gets edgy if you linger at your table long into the summer night.

YORKVILLE

Pho Hung Vietnamese Restaurant

200 Bloor Street West (west of Avenue Road)

TELEPHONE:
(416) 963-5080

CARDS:
Visa

HOURS:
Monday to Saturday:
11 a.m. to 10 p.m.

Closed Sunday

OTHER LOCATION:
350 Spadina Avenue
(416) 593-4274

The red cow logo of Pho Hung Vietnamese Restaurant — run by husband and wife Thoi and Rang — is a familiar fixture in Chinatown. Now there's an offspring, on Bloor right across from the ROM, run by Rang. Walk up two floors along a mirrored stairway to a pleasant room that seats about 75. Unless you have a fear of heights, the best seats are those along the window facing Bloor Street.

Try some exciting new tastes. A generous appetizer of about half a dozen fried frogs comes on a bed of lettuce and tomato. Limbs spread, they're about the size of the palm of your hand (your average frog size), and they're skinned, cleaned, and deep-fried in a crunchy batter. They taste like chicken. For seasoning, the server brings a little bowl of ground salt and pepper and a squeeze of lime. There's a selection of 15 different noodle soups to choose from and 11 beef soups. A steaming bowl of rare and well-done beef slices, beef balls, noodles, and rice is a meal. Everything comes in two sizes, and polite servers make recommendations: curried shrimp with coconut milk on rice, fried white fish filet with nuoc mam sauce and ginger. The fruit or vegetable milkshakes — mango, soursop, coconut, and tomato — are refreshing. Take-out is also available. Nice people. Good food.

Remy's

115 Yorkville Avenue

TELEPHONE:
(416) 968-9429

CARDS:
All major credit cards

HOURS:
Every day:
11:30 a.m. to 2 a.m.

(Kitchen closes at
11 p.m.)

Remy's is what summer in the city is all about: dishful thinking on the romantic rooftop terrace, snacking alfresco on the sidewalk patio, sipping a frosty drink at the comfy bar, or indulging in hip hop in the small and sexy video–disco, surrounded by laughter, music, and sidelong glances. A trivial pursuit — and yet, without it, summer would be like winter.

Kitchen-wise, chefs stir-fry, toss, grill, and sauté with panache, but quality and flavours have their highs and lows. Tomato and bocconcini salad or fresh tomato bruschetta are good to share. Huge coconut-rolled, deep-fried shrimps with garlic teriyaki sauce or grilled chicken breast topped with chunky Thai peanut and coriander sauce over rice noodles and vegetables are sometimes awfully good, sometimes just awful. Desserts include Nutty Buddy cheesecake, pecan pie, and fresh berries, and young servers seem really intent on our having a good time. Do it! Too soon, alas, the summer sun goes down.

Spuntini

116 Avenue Road (south of Davenport)

TELEPHONE:
(416) 962-1110

CARDS:
All major credit cards

HOURS:
Lunch:
Monday to Friday:
11 a.m. to 2:30 p.m.

Dinner:
Sunday to Wednesday:
5 p.m. to 10 p.m.

Thursday and Friday:
5 p.m. to 10:30 p.m.

Saturday:
5 p.m. to 11 p.m.

In an era when the only constant is change, the building that houses Spuntini is on the cutting edge. The room is casual and decorated in lilac and marine blue, the colours that analysts tell us will be popular for the next few years. But we don't need an analyst to tell us what good food is, or to tell us that the prices are a throwback to the sixties. Caesar salad comes in two sizes and the salad Caprese is more than generous. Dip fresh bread in herb-infused olive oil — they bring it by the bottle.

These folks are into sharing. Antipasto plates for two are almost a meal, and they're all served with gardiniera and bread. The mixed meats include prosciutto, capicolla, and salami, and come with bocconcini and provolone cheese. A plate of mixed seafood holds shrimp, mussels, anchovies, smoked salmon, and more. Servers help you pick your favourite pasta from the list. No charge for the pasta, but the sauce of your choice — Bolognese, primavera, frutti di mare (chock-full of large shrimp and scallops) — is priced accordingly. There's a gimmick in ordering pizza, too. Start with the crust, around $2, and build from a list of toppings and sauces that includes your favourite veggies, cheeses, meats, and fish. The large, thick-crust pizza is still a bargain after you've created it. Cappuccino and gelato finish the meal nicely, and since it all costs so little, you can stroll over to the pool table for a leisurely after-dinner game.

Index